#1 Best-Selling author, Dr. Kaplan is one of the most highly endorsed authors—ever! Dr. Kaplan and his books have been highly acclaimed and endorsed by such people as Donald Trump, Tom McMillen, Brian Tracy, Marla Maples, Kathy Coover, Norman Vincent Peale, Mark Victor Hansen, Duane Clemmons, Ken Blanchard, Patch Adams, Les Brown, Jack Canfield, Wally "Famous" Amos, Rudy Ruettiger, and many, many more.

Here are just a few of the many endorsements
for Dr. Kaplan's latest and best book ever:

The 5 Minute Motivator

The 5 Minute Motivator offers a practical, unique approach to experience greater success and happiness. This book will help you appreciate the blessings in your life.

Marci Shimoff, #1 New York Times Best-Selling author
Love for No Reason and Happy for No Reason

This wonderful book shows you how to become a totally positive person every day and accomplish more than you ever thought possible "5 Minutes" at a time.

Brian Tracy, Professional Speaker, Best-Selling Author of more
than 40 books, Business/Life Coach, Sales Trainer
CEO of Brian Tracy International™

Dr. Kaplan continues to educate and motivate—300 seconds at a time. His new book, The 5 Minute Motivator provides a magical stairway to a life changing experience. Success is about knowing who you are, believing in yourself and applying the principles, techniques and systems, he has so carefully provided the reader in his new book. If you are looking to be the best you can be, this book will change your life 5 minutes at a time.

Dr. Fabrizio Mancini, President, Parker University and Parker
Seminars, Author of *The Power of Self-Healing*

The tools and insights that Dr. Kaplan shares in his book, The 5 Minute Motivator are instrumental for anyone hoping to achieve their life's goals. This book will teach you how to make things happen and get results in life, "5 minutes" at a time. If you are looking for positive change in your life, this book of enlightening materials should be a must for your library.

Dr. Joe Rubino, Best-selling author of 9 books, including
31 Ways to Champion Children to Develop High Self-Esteem

The 5 Minute Motivator is a slam dunk for anyone who wants to reboot their life. Dr. Kaplan's prescriptions are time honored—the power of the mind to change our lives. As the Bible and Dr. Kaplan teach us, "What you sow in your thoughts, will determine what you reap in life". This book is a must read.

Tom McMillen, Former Congressman and Chairman of President's
Council on Sports and Physical Fitness and 11-year NBA veteran

Is it possible to invest 300 seconds with a book and receive a life-changing idea that can redirect your life? Such a book is Dr. Eric Kaplan's, The 5 Minute Motivator. As the co-founder of a dynamic growing company, thousands of associates and customers look to me for direction and motivation. So who motivates the motivator? Dr. Kaplan motivates me.

Kathy Coover, Co-Founder, Executive Vice President
Isagenix International LLC

Dr. Eric Kaplan's, The 5 Minute Motivator is the complete guide for positive transformation! Brilliantly simple and simply brilliant. I encourage you make this book your daily helping of positivity and watch your life transform into the beautiful destiny you were meant to live.

Peggy McColl, New York Times Best-Selling Author of
Your Destiny Switch

The 5 Minute Motivator lays out a simple and powerful program for achieving your goals and dreams and triumphing over the inevitable setbacks and challenges we all experience.

Pamela Yellen, Author of the New York Times Best-Seller
Bank On Yourself: The Life-Changing Secret to Growing

No life or business is free from adversity. How we deal with that adversity will ultimately determine our success as business leaders and individuals. Eric Kaplan has faced adversity head on and grown to become a recognized leader in health, wellness and chiropractic medicine. His latest book is a must read for anyone dealing with the day to day challenges of running a business or a family. He presents a new way to look at the world which will become a powerful tool for anyone trying to harness the impact of change.

William Meyer, Chairman Meyer Jabara Hotels, Chairman of the Kravis Center for the Performing Arts, Vice Chairman of The Quantum Foundation, Recipient of the Haym Salomon Award, Serves on the Board of Overseers of the School of Social Policy and Practice at the University of Pennsylvania

As a pro athlete I sought out the best in training, nutrition, and healing and Dr. Kaplan was always the first one I would call. His life experience and formal training as a doctor made him a trusted resource for guidance throughout my career. He exposed me to non-invasive, drug free, state of the art healing that repaired me and prepared me for a career in sports wellness after 10 years in the NFL. A life-long friend, mentor, and practitioner, his lessons of life are shared in his book. His book sacks the competition, literally. It's a must read and I'll share it with my players and friends.

Duane Clemons, Vikings, Defensive Captain of Kansas City Chiefs & Cincinnatti Bengals,1996-2006

Dr. Kaplan's book will add "Time to your Life and Life to your Time."
He is one among those in the quest for immortality and in "5 Minutes" he explains the power of telomeres and their ability to turn back the clock. He touches the mental, spiritual and the physical keys to living a healthy happy life, one minute at a time; a must read for anyone who wants to be healthy, live longer and enjoy their time on this planet.

Dr. Bill Andrews, Ph.D, Telomere Scientist Founder and President, Sierra Sciences

The 5 Minute Motivator offers advice to help the reader construct a life of success and happiness.

Tony Hsieh, New York Times Best-Selling author of *Delivering Happiness* and CEO of Zappos.com, Inc.

Dr. Kaplan Talks the Talk and Walks the Walk, literally. After being 100% paralyzed and making a miraculous recovery, he understands what it takes to win. His will and positive mental attitude are displayed in the pages of his new book, The 5 Minute Motivator. As a professional athlete, I understand the inner winner we all must reach for to succeed in life. Dr. Kaplan's book Awakens the Winner in us all. This book is a must read. I highly recommend it,

Mark McNulty, PGA Tour Professional, winner of 58 events, including 5 Majors, Senior PGA Championship, Senior British Open Championship, US Senior Open, Senior Players Championship

I love Dr. Eric Kaplan's new book, The 5 Minute Motivator, for its simplicity and yet profound impact on one's life. It is truly an inspirational book for many

Ping Li, Best-Selling Author of *Awakening: Fulfilling Your Soul's Purpose on Earth*

Dr. Kaplan's new book The 5 Minute Motivator will WOW you "5 Minutes" at a time. He challenges the reader while delivering his message. A must for anyone who wants to get the most out of their life. Dr. Kaplan makes you realize if you see the invisible in life, you can do the impossible.

Dr. Gerry Mattia, President Discforce, Inc., President Energy Vitality Former President International Chiropractic Association Council on Sports and Physical Fitness

A powerful guide to living life well, The 5 Minute Motivator proves that time invested in our truest purpose is indeed time well-spent.

Christine Louise Hohlbaum, Best-Selling author of *The Power of Slow: 101 Ways to Save Time in Our 24/7 World*

Dr. Kaplan's new book, The 5 Minute Motivator will help you gain a renewed and vivid appreciation of life, minute by minute. The book offers a "tool kit" that will infuse your brain with a new sense of aliveness and possibility.

Anat Baniel, Clinical Psychologist and Best-Selling Author of *Move Into Life* and *Kids Beyond Limits*

Dr. Kaplan's book provides not only the empirical formula to winning and success, but he provides you with a map, "5 Minutes" at a time. His skills as a teacher, educator, and motivator are second to none. This book is must read for anyone looking to reach their full potential.

Tom Ness, Golf Professional, Author Golf Digest, Recognized by Golf Digest as one of the Top 50 golf instructors in the United States

The search is over! Finally the magic pill of "plug and play" motivation exists today. Much more than a booster shot of motivation, Dr. Kaplan's game plan to success is the simplest, easiest, most concise and direct strategy to bring out the BEST in each one of us. My only regret is I didn't have access to it years ago. The 5 Minute Motivator will serve as the master plan in laying our personal course to our #1 desire to achieve, to become and to WIN!

Dr. Perry Bard, CEO Concierge Coaches

Dr. Kaplan has written another life-changing book. The 5 Minute Motivator is a powerful and comprehensive guide to success and happiness that anyone at any age can experience. His book will help you build the life of love and happiness "300 Seconds" at a time. Thank you. Eric, for this important, life-changing book."If you want to experience inner fulfillment on a whole new level, read this book."

Dr. Stuart Hoffman, Amazon #1 Best-Selling author of *I AM a Lovable ME!*

As an author, teacher and businesswomen, I will incorporate your lessons into daily ideas for living. I found your book uplifting and motivating. Your book is a gift that keeps on giving.

Catherine MacDonald, #1 Amazon Best-selling author of *The Way*

Dr. Kaplan has done it again—he motivates, inspires and entertains the reader throughout the entire book. This book is simply awesome. It's loaded with good values and lessons that every person should instill in their lives.

Jacki Baskow, CEO Baskow and Associates

What does it take to engage all your senses in a journey to discover your richest, most fulfilling life? According to author Dr. Eric Kaplan, it only takes 5 minutes! The deceptively simple premise—and sheer genius—of **The 5-Minute Motivator** *is that miracles can happen by thinking and focusing differently for only 5 minutes a day. Using this inspiring book as your daily guide to those transformative moments will become a habit that you will never want to break.*

Dr. Christine Ranck, Amazon #1 Best-Selling Co-Author of
Ignite the Genius Within

As a professional golfer I understand what it takes to win—on and off the golf course. Dr. Kaplan has written another life-changing book that can show you the way to heath and happiness. He provides the reader with a powerful and comprehensive program that anyone can employ in their life regardless or their occupation. If you want to experience happiness and success at a whole new level, read this book. It will be the best "5 Minutes" you will ever invest in yourself.

Dana Quigley, PGA Golf Professional, winner of 29 events,
2005 Champions Tour, Player of The Year 2005

Dr. Eric Kaplan's, **The 5 Minute Motivator** *shows us that the fulfillment which we so eagerly seek is actually just a few steps away. Through incredibly simple exercises, Dr. Kaplan helps us realize that we can achieve what we dream, inspire others to do the same, and that abundance already exists in each of our lives. It's up to us to recognize it. Pick up this book whenever you have a few spare minutes and allow it to replenish your positivity and reactivate your drive for life.*

Dr. Carmen Harra, Clinical psychologist, intuitive counselor, and
best-selling author of *Everyday Karma and Wholeliness*

It is said that 'a people without a vision perish.' In **The 5 Minute Motivator**, *Dr. Eric Kaplan takes you on an incredible journey where he unveils your inner gifts and unravels hidden mysteries to enable you to think with a winning mind and experience the dreams you've long desired.*

Ken Lang, Author of Walking Among the Dead

The 5 Minute Motivator is a book for everyone who wishes to live their dream, inspire their children, and touch the lives of all who they know. If you wish to change your life and elicit the greatness within, then The 5 Minute Motivator by Dr. Eric Kaplan is the book to launch your success with. Every parent should share the wisdom in this book with the people they value most—their children. I loved my experience in reading this book!

Dr. Ted Brooks, Ph.D., MS., Nutrition
Isagenix Millionaire

Dr. Kaplan has certainly hit the nail on the head with his latest work, The 5 Minute Motivator. There are times in life when we need to be reminded of our strengths and that it's okay to reach for our goals in life regardless of our age. I would recommend this book to everyone, young and old, who wants to get more out of their circumstances in life.

Dr. Ken Simpson, DC, 2009 IsaBody Challenge
Grand Prize Winner

Dr. Kaplan is someone for whom I have tremendous respect and admiration. As Mrs. United States 2005 and a cosmetic dentist, I see everyday how lives are transformed for the better based simply by how someone feels about themselves. Dr. Kaplan clearly has a gift that aids people in finding that place where life takes on a much brighter rainbow and beautiful outlook.

Dr. Chiann Fan Gibson, Mrs. United States 2005

Dr. Kaplan's book is more than highly motivational. It shows you how to simply and elegantly remove mental toxins, naturally. It's mandatory reading for anyone who wants to live a healthy, happy life.

Beth Greer, Best-Selling author *Super Natural Home and Environmental Health Consultant*

If you are looking for a shot of inspiration read, The 5 Minute Motivator is a must read book. Dr. Eric Kaplan offers great tips to keep us on top of "the game of life."

Caroline Sutherland, Best-Selling Author of
The Body Knows... How to Stay Young

Dr. Kaplan offers his readers the opportunity to convert dreams into goals, change goals into plans, and live the life they've always wanted. He then delivers on his promise by offering practical advice, powerful stories, and needed inspiration... all in 5-minute bite-size pieces.

Joshua Becker, Author of #1 Best-Selling book, *Simplify*

As a firm believer in the power of believing in oneself, I was overjoyed to read a success story in which a small amount of time set aside every day, as little as 5 minutes, can command worlds of success. As proud as I am to endorse this book, I am even more gratified to know that its message will help and inspire others.

Michelle Franklin, Award-winning fantasy and romance author
Creator of *The Haanta Series*

The 5 Minute Motivator inspires anyone and everyone to be better—"5 Minutes" at a time. His words elegantly and spiritually compel the reader to look at the blessings of living, laughing, loving, and learning. A fun and powerful read.

Anna Maria Prezio, Author of #1 Best-Selling book
Confessions of a Feng Shui Ghost-Buster

The 5 Minute Motivator might be an understatement. This is a 5-minute life changer! While each snippet requires only 5 minutes to read, they contain a day's worth of digestion. There is so much power in each story and the quotations are inspiring and thoughtful. A great way to start each day that all rolls into an abundant life! How cool is that!

Carl Bozeman, Amazon Best-Selling author of
On Being God - Beyond Your Life's Purpose

In the game of life, there is no playbook to winning better than Dr. Kaplan's new book, The 5 Minute Motivator. This book will take you on an adventure to success, 300 seconds at a time, I will share this book my staff, my friends, and my family. I know it will change and enhance their lives as much as it has mine.

Carlos Becerra, CEO North America Medical

I am lucky in that I interact with Dr. Eric Kaplan frequently and am always amazed by his clear and most helpful insights about how to deal in a positive way with life's many problems. Don't miss the opportunity to learn from his approach to healthy living. This book gets to the point—clear, precise, direct. If you want to reach your potential as a person this book is the empirical guide. A must read.

Joseph Littenberg, Senior Partner Lerner, David, Littenberg, Krumholz, and Mentlik, Recognized As the Best IP Counselor

The 5 Minute Motivator is a must read for any leader. Just setting aside 5 minutes per day for personal growth can be life-altering. Many pearls of wisdom are jammed-packed in this book with most of them told in parable stories which are memorable. Well worth the price of admission, I highly recommend that you also take a ride on this book adventure.

Sam Santiago, PMP, Amazon Best-Selling Author of *The Official Book of Innovation*

Dr. Kaplan's book proves that in life you should never, ever, Give Up On Love. His book is more than highly motivational, it is inspirational. In an interval of only "5 Minutes" he helps the reader remove mental barriers that exist in life, in a natural and positive manner. I would consider this book essential reading for anyone who wants to live a healthy, happier, and more loving life. It is simple to understand and elegantly written. This book can help transform anyone, enabling them to reach their potential and fulfill their dreams.

Tim Carroll, Best-Selling Author of *Don't Ever Give Up On Love*

Our teachers and parents repeatedly told us the "keys to success." They said, "Stay focused! Concentrate! Play to your strengths!" Dr. Kaplan's, The 5 Minute Motivator teaches you how to VISUALIZE your success and confidently unlock your natural potential. The old phrases will now have new meaning because The 5 Minute Motivator shows you how to comfortably make these concepts part of your way of life and stay one step ahead of the competition!

Ira Sherman, Managing Partner, Chaikin, Sherman, Cammarata and Siegel, P.C., Past Pres., D.C. Trial Lawyers Ass'n.

THE 5 MINUTE MOTIVATOR

DR. ERIC KAPLAN

RED WILLOW PUBLISHING

Cover Design by Steve Wilson
www.insightpublishing.com

Red Willow Books
www.RedWillowBooks.com

The 5 Minute Motivator
www.5minutemotivator.com

In Memory...

Dr. Donald Gutstein was my professor, my mentor, and my friend. He turned boys into men, girls into women, and men and women into doctors. I am grateful for all that I am, realizing this man helped make me the man that I am; I will miss him.

I am also grateful to so many family members I've lost that have inspired me throughout my life, including my parents Elsie & Mike Kaplan, for making my life and success possible. To all my grandparents, for their love, belief, and support.

To my aunts and uncles Diane Adler, Herbert Punyon, Vivian Daniels, and cousins Doris & Milton Garfunkel, Norman Roth, Lou, Al, Marty & Dick Brenner, Jerome Shapiro, and Ruth Zuck.

*I dedicate this book to my two sons, **Michael Kaplan** and **Jason Kaplan**, my future healers. I am hoping the stories in this book will be passed from generation to generation. You both motivate me and inspire me to be my best. I love you both.*

Acknowledgements

I want to acknowledge my wife, my muse of 31 years—Bonnie Kaplan—whose patience and understanding has been a blessing.

My brother Steven Kaplan and his wife Gloria Kaplan, I am blessed to have these people in my life to share my life.

To my entire family—aunts, uncles, cousins—for their love and support.

To all my friends, for being my friends.

I especially want to acknowledge the elders of my family. My Aunt Gloria Punyon has been there for me my entire life. She is my second mother and has always inspired me and believed in everything I ever did. To my Uncle Herbert "Buddy" Adler, who spent his life with class and dignity and always led by example. Growing up with their families, Amy, Ellen, Joel, and Jerry are memories I will always cherish.

To my other uncle, Milton Daniels, and cousins who I love like uncles and aunts: Jack Segall, Milton and Linda Siegel, Jerome and Barbara Levine, Maxine Shapiro, and Phil Zuck.

TABLE OF CONTENTS

The 5 Minute Motivator

Success is based on attitude, and attitude can be altered by time. We are all born with an equal inheritance of approximately 700,000 hours. One of the great differences between life and death is that life offers us a choice, while death offers a mystery. We have a choice of how we live these 700,000 hours and we can choose the quality of our existence on this journey of life. Many people live their lives in a whirlpool, marred by confusion, and absent of direction on their quest to succeed. Man and woman were born to succeed. It's the goal of this book to continually activate endorphins by turning your basic coffee break into a 5 minute motivator. In "5 minutes" or less, simply by reading any chapter in this book, you can alter your being, alter your existence, transform your dreams into realities, and have your realities create dreams for other people. This book will offer a series of vignettes, motivational techniques, and stories that will teach you the secrets of success. The 5 Minute Motivator is a proven system that will unlock your powers to succeed.

This book contains an empirical formula to personal success that introduces a synergy of methods and ideas, techniques, and motivational anecdotes—all brought together in one place. Each individual component can be learned and revisited in just "5 minutes" a day. The principles of success, health, and happiness are not new. The concept of the 5 minute motivator is to embellish these principles into a user-friendly system that maintains your interest while providing a winning strategy: Winning at the game of life.

Life is based on numbers: the seconds in a minute, the minutes in an hour, hours in a day, days in a week, weeks in a month, months in a year, and years in a life. The human body consists of approximately one trillion cells, which work 24 hours a day, 7 days a week, 365 days a year, never taking a vacation, let alone a minute off. When you stop to consider that the human body is perfect—that a heart beats an average of 72 times per minute, which is approximately 100,000 times per day, over 700,000 times per week, almost 3 million times per month, and over 34 million times per year—and never takes a minute off—you realize that our life is dictated by time. We need to utilize time efficiently to experience all life has to offer. Life is like a combination lock, only with more numbers. If you select the right numbers in the right sequence, you can unlock the treasure chest of health, happiness, and success. In "5 minutes" you can be the locksmith of your destiny. It takes just "5 minutes" to change your psychology, alter your physiology, and transform you into the person that you were born to be. The only way to break a bad habit is simply to drop it. What we need to do is create healthy, happy, and positive habits. In just 5 minutes, a minimum of once a day, The 5 minute Motivator will provide the techniques that can literally transform your destiny. Imagine if success could be obtained in only 5 minutes!

Walt Disney said, "Your imagination creates your reality." Close your eyes. Look into your subconscious, your inner eye. What do you see? Like an architect, you must create the blueprints of your life. Imagine you could be anywhere you wished—on an island, in the mountains, maybe even at sea. Transport yourself wherever you wish. Smell the air. Feel the sun and the wind. Hear the birds. See yourself smiling, at peace, and happy. Picture yourself as you want to be.

Now, I ask you: How did you get to this place? You put yourself there through your imagination. Visualization will create reality. With this realization, you have learned the first key to unlocking your inner dreams—your imagination will create your reality.

My wife and I came back from the dead. We looked death in the eye and said, "It's not my time." We have come to treasure life and our time on this planet. Life is for living, laughing, loving, and learning, not whining, worrying, and working.

Life is a grindstone. Whether it grinds us down or polishes us up depends on us.

Thomas L. Holdcroft

Chapter 1

Life is Difficult

M. Scott Peck, MD sold over five million copies of his book, *The Road Less Traveled*. What I remember most from reading this book are the first three words: Life is difficult. Is that a positive or negative thought, or is it just a fact? We must all recognize that success does not follow the path of least resistance, that words can be substituted for other words, and that words do not have to control our mindset. It's the thoughts we create, the visions we apply while reading these words that define our lives and put up obstacles to that success.

In 5 minutes, or 300 seconds, you can control your mind and your life by accepting your circumstances and by changing your attitude.

My wife and I were completely paralyzed after cosmetic injections. We weren't able to move a muscle in our bodies, not even to open our eyes. The doctors and nurses weren't sure at times if we were alive or dead. Our prognosis was grim. Would we survive, and if we did, what condition we would be in? We were expected to live our lives in wheelchairs, possibly on ventilators. They advised us to change our lives and either sell our home or make it wheelchair accessible. We were facing difficult times ahead and we needed to find a way back to life, a road to recovery, a road to success, health, and happiness. We found it once we knew God would not abandon us in our time of need. We needed faith and we needed to work harder than we had ever worked. We needed to believe more then we have ever believed. It started daily during rehab with our mindset. All people have obstacles—even the President of the United States has obstacles—but change is about turning obstacles into challenges

Can we, transform "life is difficult" to "life is a challenge"? Of course we can. Life is full of challenges. Life is about choices. Every day we make choices. The key is to make the right choices. You can be a winner or a loser, happy or unhappy, healthy or sick, a victor or a victim, apt or inept, willing or unwilling, strong or weak. James Allen, author of the best-selling book, *As A Man Thinketh*, said, "A person is limited only by the thoughts that he chooses." He also stated, "The outer conditions of a person's life will always be found to be harmoniously related to his inner state...Men do not attract that which they want, but that which they are."

We must take the plunge into life. Life cannot consist of indecision and second-guessing. We must be more than average, average is defined as *the best of the worst and the worst of the best!* There is no middle ground in life. We must not be scared to be who we are or think what we think. We must not be frozen by our fears. These are the mortal enemies of spontaneous brilliance. We must not forsake our uniqueness to become a carbon copy of the Madonna's and the Michael Jackson's of the world. We must utilize our uniqueness, and through this uniqueness create spontaneity.

> *Without action, your dreams, goals, or plans will have little meaning to the world. The dreamers are the saviors of the world. As the visible world is sustained by the invisible, so men, through all their trials and sins and sordid vocations, are nourished by the beautiful visions of their solitary dreamers.*
>
> **James Allen**

Living and risking are very close companions. If you sense that you've made a good decision, have faith and move forward. A wise man once said, "If you put everything off until you are sure of it, you will get nothing done." You don't have to take life the way it comes to you. You have the ability to move away or to step back. You have the ability to set goals and to make affirmations. Life is for the living, and dreaming creates reality. What if Edison didn't see the light, Morse didn't hear the code, or Graham didn't hear the bell? What if the Wright brothers were wrong? What if Galileo wasn't a night owl? What if Columbus didn't like to sail? What if Einstein didn't like math or didn't have the time?

By converting your dreams into goals and your goals into plans, you can design your life to come to you the way you want it. You can live your life on purpose instead of by chance. Allow yourself the freedom to grow and develop the habit of saying yes to your own potential. Take the time to think of all the reasons why you can, and why you will excel at something wonderful, because there will always be plenty of people around you to tell you why you can't. It takes just "5 minutes" to dig in to your subconscious spirit—to your soul—and transform your being. You must have a positive thought for every day—an inner core, an inner saying, a mantra. A lack of opportunity is driven by a lack of vision. Go for the opportunity!

> *Cherish your visions; cherish your ideals; cherish the music that stirs in your heart, the beauty that forms in your mind, the loveliness that drapes your purest thoughts, and if you but remain true to them, your world will at last be built.*
> **James Allen**

The road you choose in life will only be as strong and as powerful as your attitude. How you see the world is how the world will see you. Are you a positive person? Are you willing to spend "5 minutes" per day to change your life, to give yourself the life you have always dreamed of, the life you deserve? Or are you going to do the same thing, the same way and expect a different result? You were put on this earth to do something wonderful with your life. Your job is to find out what that wonderful thing is and then throw your whole heart into doing it extremely well.

One day a traveler was walking along a road on his journey from one village to another. As he walked he noticed a monk tending the ground in the fields beside the road. The monk said "Good day" to the traveler, and the traveler nodded to the monk.

The traveler then turned to the monk and said, "Excuse me, do you mind if I ask you a question?"

"Not at all," replied the monk.

"I am traveling from the village in the mountains to the village in the valley and I was wondering if you knew what it is like in the village in the valley?"

"Tell me," said the monk, "What was your experience of the village in the mountains?"

"Dreadful," replied the traveler, "to be honest I am glad to be away from there. I found the people most unwelcoming. When I first arrived I was greeted coldly. I was never made to feel part of the village no matter how hard I tried. The villagers keep very much to themselves; they don't take kindly to strangers. So tell me, what can I expect in the village in the valley?"

"I am sorry to tell you," said the monk, "but I think your experience will be much the same there".

The traveler hung his head despondently and walked on.

Later that same day, another traveler was journeying down the same road and he also came upon the monk.

"I'm going to the village in the valley," said the second traveler, "Do you know what it is like?"

"I do," replied the monk "But first tell me, where have you come from?"

"I've come from the village in the mountains."

"And how was that?"

"It was a wonderful experience. I would have stayed if I could, but I'm committed to traveling on. I felt as though I was a member of the family in the village. The elders gave me much advice, the children laughed and joked with me and people were generally kind and generous. I am sad to have left there. It will always hold special memories for me. And what of the village in the valley?" he asked again.

"I think you will find it much the same" replied the monk, "Good day to you".

"Good day and thank you," the traveler replied, smiled, and journeyed on.

In life, as the Monk revealed in the story above, your attitude will carry you from town to town, person to person, and situation to situation. Your attitude can be altered by simply altering your way of thinking. We're all masters of our own thoughts, our own destiny. Our thoughts are the seeds to our actions, our actions are the seeds to our future. Plant your seeds of positive thinking daily and watch your dreams grow.

By seeing yourself the way you want to be, you can become this person. Spend "5 minutes" each day believing in yourself, believing that you can leap barriers and achieve your goals—that is the ticket to success. One of the most powerful tools for building self-confidence is visualization.

Once you decide what you want in life, simply visualize yourself having it. Visualization helps you use your mind and your natural creative imagination to actually manifest those things that you wish to achieve most in your life. This is a very powerful technique that for centuries has been proven to work.

To harness the power of visualizations you must truly believe in its amazing power to work in your life. If you don't have true belief in your heart you will sabotage any attempts you make toward achieving total success. With a positive mindset and a positive attitude you can bring about wonderful events in your life. However, If you call yourself stupid, or say you are miserable or unlucky or any such negative term or statement you will begin to visualize those things and sure enough they will become true in your life. This book will take you on a journey to success "5 minutes" at a time. James Allen said " Man's mind may be likened to a garden, which may be intelligently cultivated or allow to run wild; but whether cutivated or neglected, it must, and will, bring forth. If no useful seeds are put into it, then an abudance of useless weed-seeds will fall therin, and will continue to produce their kind."

What you think about, comes about, people that think positive, that compliment themselves and expect good things to occur are more likely to develop an image in their mind to match what they say to themselves. I call self talk affirmations. Affirmations defined briefly is positive self talk. Fact is we all talk to ourselves, so keep your self-talk positive, reassuring and always expecting the best out of every situation in life. Use self talk and visualization with very strong emotions to create a vivid image of your goals if life as if they were already accomplished. The very act of visualization bringing about wonderful events in your life has occurred without you being aware. You visualized yourself walking before you ever walked, you visualized yourself falling in love, before you ever fell in love. Some people call it coincidence but there is no such thing as coincidence in this world. We are responsible for what happens to us throughout our lives.

Our brain and our mind are the most powerful forces on this Earth and the more we learn to use them to our positive advantage the better our lives can be. You can change your circumstances and accomplishments in your life just by thinking about them and creating a true and strong, vivid images of what it is you desire

My mantra is: Whatever it takes. The road to success is always under construction and in life there's no free ride. This road to success often has many detours. But you can spend just "5 minutes"—only 300 seconds a day—visualizing whatever you want in life. Choose your dream job, car, relationship, house, or family. Each day, like an architect, design your dream life. Think about the materials you will need, the time it will take to build this life, the site of your new life. You are the architect of your dreams, your destiny.

Just imagine if God said, "Be the architect of your life. You can become whatever you design." Now, realize you are. Life supplies us with all the tools, materials, and abilities that are needed. It's now up to you to develop the blueprints and build your future. It takes as little as "5 minutes" to plant the seeds of success that will lead to a fruitful harvest of greatness that lies within your spirit. If you plant your dreams into your heart, spirit, and soul, their roots will anchor your vision and create your reality.

I must govern the clock, not be governed by it.

Golda Meir

Chapter 2

The Awakening

Join me as we enter my time machine and revisit the past. The mind is an amazing instrument, for it harbors the ability to turn the present into the past, the past into the present, or the present into the future. Today, let's take "5 minutes" and take control of your present and move your success to the future, while we learn from the past.

The past is history, the future is a mystery, but this moment right here and right now is a gift, which is why we call it the "*present*." Our goal in this chapter is to unwrap our gift and make use of our present, this moment, and the next "5 minutes."

You see, once you started this chapter you opened my time machine. Whatever happened in your past is done and over with. Don't hang on to bad memories, learn from the past and move on. You can't undo your past, so once we accept it, we are able to move on and enjoy our "Present." I'm sorry if someone hurt your feelings, but dwelling on the past will not help your future. Our future can be determined by our present mindset, what we think, feel and do right here, right now is the gift of life.

Nobody gets to live life backward. Look ahead, that is where your future lies.

Ann Landers

Let me take you to the past and introduce you to Henry Ford. Henry Ford had very little schooling, yet he was a highly educated man because he acquired the ability to combine natural and economic premises and he understood the value of resources. He recognized that by masterminding with brilliant men, he had the ability to achieve anything he wanted. But, as often happens, there were always those who would steal his thunder or try to conform his unconformable spirit.

During World War I, Ford brought suit against the *Chicago Tribune* because that publication had called him an ignoramus, an ignorant pacifist. When the suit came to trial, the *Tribune*'s lawyers wanted to prove that Henry Ford was, in fact, ignorant. As the story goes, during cross-examination the question was asked, "How many soldiers did the British send over to subdue the rebellion of the colonies in 1776?" With a grin, Mr. Ford replied, "I do not know just how many, but I have heard it was a lot more than ever went back." Of course, this brought raucous laughter to the courtroom and enraged the opposing counsel. This line of interrogation continued for more than an hour, with the defense attorneys asking meaningless questions designed to discredit Mr. Ford. The barrage of questions was obnoxious and insulting. Nevertheless, Ford sat calmly throughout the entire performance. Finally, he stood up and pointed a finger at the interrogating attorney and said, "If I should really wish to answer the foolish question you have just asked, or any other that you have been asking, let me remind you that I have row of electric pushbuttons hanging over my desk. And, by placing my finger on the right button, I could call in men who could give the correct answer to all the questions that you have asked, and too many that you have neither the intelligence to ask, nor to answer. Now, sir, will you kindly tell me why I should bother filling my head with useless details in order to answer every foolish question that anyone may ask, when I have able men about me who can supply me with all the facts I want when I call for them?"

There was a silence in the courtroom. The questioning attorney's jaw dropped as his eyes opened wide. The judged leaned forward and stared Ford directly in the eyes. The jury awoke as if an explosion had just occurred. And Henry Ford won his case. He proved to all that education comes with the development of one's mind and the utilization and implementation of resources. No, he could not name the capitols of each state, but he taught the world that one man can intelligently use the knowledge possessed by another for his own gain. The man who embraces this understanding is as much or more educated as the man who merely possesses knowledge, but does not know what to do with it. Let us utilize our resources.

We live in a world filled with an abundance of resources. We are so concerned with the pursuit of wealth that we often fail to recognize how wealthy we already are. This is because many of us attribute our wealth to personal holdings (how big is my house, my property, my bank account, etc.). Yet, we don't realize the many other resources we own. In this great country, we have the ability to go to parks, beaches, wilderness preserves—thousands of acres that we all own. Yes, in many of these national historic sites there is an entrance fee, but if you personally owned this property, what would your daily upkeep and taxes cost? What about libraries? What about the Internet? We live in a land with an abundance of knowledge in which we can access the best of the world's minds, all in a matter of "5 minutes." Our life is not defined by personal property or things. We are so consumed with selfish idealism that we forget the abundant realism that surrounds us. Life is not about yours and mine— life is about ours. Why buy an estate just to gate it off and isolate yourself from others? We work to accumulate possessions that we hoard, while life's real treasures reside in abundance everywhere around us. "Public" means yours, mine, and ours. Why limit yourself to what you can buy then limit others to sharing?

Take "5 minutes" today, and every day forward, to enjoy the abundance that is yours. Take a walk on a beach or in a park. See a museum or visit a library. Realize as you visualize that the treasures of the world are at your fingertips, within your grasp. They are just "5 minutes" away!

Maxwell Maltz, the author of *Psycho-Cybernetics*, said that if you do something for 21 consecutive days, it becomes a habit. For example, if you read something positive for "5 minutes" every day for 21 days, it will become habit. Let's spend the next "5 minutes" studying my ways to make every day a happy day.

"5 Minute" Ways to Have a Great Day Today

1. **Wake Up "5 Minutes" Earlier Than Normal**
   Get up "5 minutes" before the alarm goes off and take the first "5 minutes" for yourself. Exercise, meditate, set your daily goals, say your affirmations, and hug your spouse or loved one and your family. Read a poem, enjoy the sunrise. Spend "5 minutes" setting your goals. Once we get busy and into our daily routine, there never seems to be enough time in the day for ourselves.

2. **Read, Listen, and Watch Something Uplifting**
   We are inundated by the media. Make positive choices with the books you read and the shows you watch. Positive things in any form will uplift your spirit. Read your affirmations and make this a daily "5 minute" habit. A great day does not begin with the negative news we see on our televisions, listen to on the radio, or read in our newspapers. Great days begin with great ideas, with great energy.

3. **A Healthy Breakfast Will Start Your Day Off Right**
   I start my day with a protein shake; it takes less than "5 minutes." (Go to my web site www.5minutemotivator.com to learn more about my healthy living habits.) Lets start our day with healthy foods in our body. Protein comes from the Greek word *proteus*, meaning "of prime importance." Think about the energy our bodies need to perform on any given day. Life is not a race, it's a marathon. What would you need to eat and drink to win it?

4. **Awaken Your Winning Attitude**
   Your attitude is the first choice you make every day. Spend

your first "5 minutes" each day awakening the winning attitude within yourself. Don't let your attitude come between you and your success. Be careful to keep it positive all day long. A good attitude and a good smile will make for a winning day.

5. **Listen to Family and Friends**
   My father once said, "God gave you two ears and one mouth for a reason." Listen to the people around you because they'll have a profound effect on how you get through life. Our closest friends and family are our greatest environmental influences. Make sure you have the best advisors you can find and when you find them, listen.

6. **Make the Most of Every Day**
   Start each day in a positive way. When you get to your work, make it the best place to be not only for yourself, but those around you. Learn to appreciate every second, every minute, every hour of every day. Make your work place a happier place. So many of us go to work and never think about making the office a fun and happy place. Raise the spirit of your office and a raise is in your future, as well. Focus on your contribution. What would it be like if you were not around? Make yourself irreplaceable. Give 100% each and every day.

7. **Always Remember the Walls Have Ears**
   Make a point of speaking well of others. Wish others the best in life and they will do the same for you. Remember, what goes around does come around. Don't talk negative about anyone. Try to understand them as individuals and be aware of their life and their circumstances. Practice being a support system to your friends and family and co-workers. The world needs you.

8. **Be Fair and Honest with Everyone**
   Honesty does make a difference. Ethics goes a long way and you only have one name—make it a good one. What you give to others is usually what you get from others. Practice integrity that people can see, sense, and feel. Always make a conscious effort to be aware of what you say and how you say it. Tone goes a long way in communication. Learn to walk your talk at all times. The more people trust you, the more of their time they will trust with you.

9. **Pace Your Energy to Last The Entire Day**
   Lets manage our energy to last a full day. Be careful of
   unnecessary bursts of energy, you don't want to burn out to
   early in the day. The key is to have something left over for your
   friends and family. Remember, you're not a candle, you have
   the ability to control the burn of your light. Pace yourself and
   your energy throughout the day. By spending "5 minutes"
   planning your entire day before you begin, you'll have what
   you need. Remember the old saying "look alive."

10. **Early To Bed Early to Rise**
    Develop the "5 minute" habit of reading positive material
    before you sleep. You can't succeed if you don't read.
    Remember, throughout the day that life is what we make it,
    day by day. Practice having the best day ever; it adds up to
    a great life. And don't forget #1—get up a "5 minutes" early
    tomorrow to start your day in a positive way.

Let us turn these ways into habits. Remember, we either have good
habits or bad habits. The best way to break a bad habit is to *drop it*. I know
it will take hard work to master the secrets to health and happiness, but
that is why you joined me on this journey and it's worth the investment
of "5 minutes" per day.

Seneca said, *"It is a rough road that leads to the heights of greatness."*
The rough road you choose can lead you to greatness. Everyone would be
wealthy if it were easy. But perhaps everyone *is* wealthy. Don't be blinded
by other people's thoughts. Within every person lives a spirit, a desire,
a mindset, a knowledge that you were put on earth for a reason. The
Sanskrit calls it a Dharma. What was God's purpose in putting you on
earth? If God's gift to man is life, then man's gift to God is what he does
with that life. You have a choice; a choice to move in any direction. Since
you do have alternatives, choose only one direction—up.

Live as if your were to die tomorrow. Learn as if you were to live forever.

Gandhi

Chapter 3

The Secret of Life

According to an ancient Greek story, a gathering of the gods took place on Mount Olympus when the world was young. Having created the earth, man, all the animals and birds, the creatures of the sea, flowers, plants, and all other living things, the gods still had one thing left to do. They had to hide the secret of life where it couldn't be found until mankind had grown and evolved in consciousness to a point where they were ready for such wisdom and understanding. The gods argued back and forth over where to hide the secret of life. One said, *"Let's hide it on the highest peak of the highest mountain. Mankind will not find it there."* But another god responded, *"We have created mankind with an insatiable thirst for knowledge, and an insatiable curiosity and ambition. It's because of these traits that he will eventually conquer the mountain and obtain the secret of life."* The gods continued to talk of mankind's strengths and weaknesses, realizing that many times a person's strength was derived from his or her weaknesses. They knew that mankind was born without the ability to climb; yet that weakness could be turned into strength because it could give the incentive to learn to climb. Man was not born knowing how to swim, a weakness. The ability to learn to swim was a strength.

"We should not underestimate the power of mankind," one god said to another. And, they continued to dialogue and make suggestions until one god suggested, *"We need to hide the secret in the deepest part of the*

deepest ocean." To this another god responded, *"That won't work. We have designed mankind with unlimited energy; a boundless imagination, and a burning desire to seek, dream, and explore the world—to succeed at all costs. Mankind's inherent ability to succeed will provide him with the ability to conquer even the greatest ocean depths."*

Finally, one of the gods came up with what he felt was the solution: *"Let us hide this in the one place where mankind will never look. A place they will only come to when they have exhausted all other possibilities and are finally ready."*

"And where will that be?" the gods chorused.

Zeus stood up and replied, *"We will hide it in the deepest part of the human heart. For mankind will not look there until he has truly evolved."*

And so they did.

Man's quest for the secret of life spans 5,000 years of recorded history and has occupied some of the world's wisest men and women, as well as some of the greatest leaders of all religions. The key that will unlock the vast treasure chest of greatness, lies deep within each person. We need to stop looking outside of ourselves for the answers, since all the answers of the universe lie somewhere within.

One unsettled man chose to enter into a journey, a quest. After looking around at what he had, he became more concerned with what he did not have. So he sold all his worldly possessions in search of the secret of life and flew to India. Upon arriving in India, the natives looked at the man and said, *"How can we help you?"*

The man said, *"I am here to find the secret of life."*

And they pointed to a local mountain and said, *"If you climb up that mountain and you ask to speak to the Maharajah Mukesh, he will tell you of the secret of life."*

So, the man picked up his gear and climbed the mountain. There, on top of the mountain in a shack surrounded by sheep, was a tattered old man whose eyes were illuminated by strength, not weakness.

The Maharajah looked at the man and asked, "*How may I help you, my son?*"

"*I am here to learn the secret of life,*" said the man.

"*My son,*" said the Maharajah, "*you have traveled all this way to learn something you already know.*"

The man looked at the Master and said, "*Maharajah, if I knew the answer, I would not ask the question.*"

"*The answer, my son, is not complex,*" answered the Master, "*but it is something you must understand. The secret of life is I AM.*"

The man was surprised and repeated, "*I am?*"

The Master looked into the traveler's tired eyes and replied, "*Yes, my son. I AM.*"

The man became irritated and retorted, "*Well, there has to be more to life than that! This is something that I already knew!*"

The Master looked at the man and said, "*But is it something that you believe?*"

The man then declared, "*You're a phony,*" and he left.

He went back down the mountain and found the man who had recommended that he seek the Master. The man fumed, "*He was no visionary! He didn't know the answer! Have you seen the way he lives? He lives amongst sheep in a broken-down shack with tattered clothes. This man could not know the secret of life!*"

The guide looked at the man and responded, "*There is only one master of equal knowledge. To see him you must travel a great distance. This journey will take ten days through the mountains, to the peak of the Himalayas.*"

So the man hired a party and for ten days he traveled through the Himalayas. On the tenth day, the sun rose as they began their march, and on the slope of the mountain ahead, the man saw one of the most beautiful temples he had ever seen, a temple that sparkled of gold and silver. The closer he got to the temple, the more impressed he became with the magnificent dwelling. He walked in and asked to meet the Master. Soon, the Master came to meet the traveler. He had silver hair, his eyes shone, and he was surrounded by an aura of peace and contentment. When he spoke, his words were gentle: *"My son, you have traveled a long way. How can I help you?"* And the man replied, *"I have come here to learn the secret of life."*

"Ah, the secret of life," said the Master. *"So many people travel to our country to learn something that they already know."*

And then the Master asked, *"Have you not already asked this question of any of the other masters along the way?"*

"Yes," said the man. *"I asked this question of the Master Mukesh, but he gave me the answer, 'I AM'. How could a man who lives on the side of a mountain, in a broken-down dwelling, surrounded by smelly sheep possibly know the answer to the secret of life?"*

The Master looked at him and spoke in a soft voice, *"My son, I see that you do not know the secret of life. I will teach it to you, but there will be a price."*

The man smiled back and said, *"Well, how much? I am prepared to pay any amount that you may ask."*

"My son," answered the Master, *"Look around you. You cannot buy the secret of life. That is an investment you must make in time. If you will spend five years living in my barn amongst my animals and be their caretaker, on the first day of the sixth year we will meet again and I will tell you the secret of life."*

The man agreed.

So, for five years the man lived within the dwelling. He milked the cows, brushed the horses, chased the goats, and swept the floors. On the first day of the sixth year, he re-entered the temple. The five years had taken quite a toll on the man. He did not appear happy. His face was pale, his eyes sullen. His hair was now gray, his posture weakened, and his teeth were discolored. He stood in front of the Master and said, *"I have done everything you have asked. I lived amongst your animals and was their caretaker for five years. Now Master, I have come on the first day of the sixth year to ask you for the secret of life."*

The Master sat down and he said, *"Give me your hand."*

The man held out his now callused hand to the Master, whose hands were soft as silk, but still suggested both strength and power, yet his hands also had warmth that emanated into the hands of the weary traveler. The Master then looked into the traveler's eyes and said, *"My son, the secret of life is hidden within. The secret of life has always been within you. The secret of life is, I AM."*

The traveler pulled his hand back, jumped up, and shouted, *"I AM? I am WHAT? I am five years older! I am five years more tired! I am five years more broken down, and you tell me something that I already know? How dare you deceive me!"*

At this point, the Master stood up and said, *"Deceive you? I never deceived you. Five years ago today you passed the Master Maharajah, who was once my master, and you looked at him and you judged him because he lived on the side of a mountain, surrounded by sheep that he adored. You asked him the secret of life and he told you, 'I AM'. But that was not good enough. It was too easy, too simple. So you came to my opulent palace and you again asked the question that had been already answered; this question whose answer existed within you. If I had given you the same answer, you would have gone on to the next, even more opulent castle, and asked the same question. But the answer remains the same: I AM, YOU ARE. You see, I am responsible for where I sit; I am responsible for everything that I have, as are you. You chose to travel to my castle; you chose to live in my barn. There were no restraints. You could have left any day you wanted, but your desire to know kept you there, and kept you going. Now, the price you paid might have been steep, but maybe this time when you leave, you will realize you chose your destiny. You chose to come to this country; you chose to live amongst my animals, and because you chose to do this, this choice led to the direction of your life and it paralleled your existence. Yes, my son, I AM. YOU ARE. The secret of life exists within each and every one of us."*

Here's the premise: We are all, right now, living the life we choose. This choice, of course, is not a single, monumental choice. The choices

I'm talking about here are made daily, hourly, moment by moment. Do we try something new, or stick to the tried-and-true? Do we take a risk, or eat what's already on our plate? Do we ponder a thrilling adventure, or contemplate what's on TV? Do we walk over and meet that interesting stranger, or do we play it safe? Do we indulge our heart, or cater to our fear? Do we pursue what we want, or do we do what's simply comfortable?

For the most part, most people choose comfort—the familiar, the time-honored, the well-worn but well-known. After a lifetime of choosing between comfort and risk, we are left with the life we currently have. We can begin a new adventure, right here, right now, and the only cost is "5 minutes" of your time. Are you ready? "I AM!"

Without goals, and plans to reach them, you are like a ship that has set sail with no destination.

Fitzhugh Dodson

Chapter 4

Navigate the Seven Cs to Success

Get ready to sail the Seven "Cs"—the Seven "Cs" to Success. Now is your time to navigate your vessel along the waters of life found in these seven "Cs." If you want to be a total success you must master these "Cs." Let's spend "5 minutes" a day sailing the Seven "Cs." As you sail through this chapter spend "5 minutes" to write down and implement the "Cs" you will now sail. If you can master the Seven "Cs," you will cruise to success.

Caring—The vitamin of friendship is B1—if you want a friend, you must *be one*. True success in this world is not just based on economic holdings, but personal relationships. We must have a bigger vision than simply accomplishing a goal for personal gain. I believe that people that find true success have a deep caring for other people. Yes, they can be a Type A personality, even aggressive, but you cannot be so tough, so aggressive, that you run roughshod over others.

Treat everyone with politeness, even those who are rude to you - not because they are nice, but because you are.

Author Unknown

Character—Becoming a success is more than increasing the digits in your bank account. In life you can always make more money, but time is limited, what you do with your time will determine your character.

Character development takes work and discipline. The key is letting each and every experience shape and mold us as we experience them. We must discipline ourselves to always be moving toward our goal and never allowing negative circumstances to destroy us but make us stronger. This is what true success is about!

The world needs men and women. . .

who cannot be bought;
whose word is their bond;
who put character above wealth;
who possess opinions and a strong will;
who are larger than their vocations;
who do not hesitate to take risks;
who will not lose their individuality in a crowd;
who will be as honest in small affairs as in greater;
who will make no compromise with wrong;
whose ambitions are not confined to their own selfish desires;
who will not say they do it "because everybody else does it;"
who are true to their friends through good and bad, in adversity as well as in prosperity;
who do not believe that shrewdness, cunning, and hardheadedness are the best qualities for winning success;
who are not ashamed or afraid to stand for the truth when it is unpopular;
who can say "no" with emphasis, although all the rest of the world says "yes."

Author Unknown

Choice—Life is about choices, each day from the time we wake up we make choices. In life, every movement you make toward your ultimate success and destiny will be because you choose to move toward it. The actions that you choose, each and every day will add up, over the long-term, to your final destination. The power we have as humans to choose is one of the greatest gifts known to mankind.

> *Every art and every inquiry, and similarly every action and choice, is thought to aim at some good; and for this reason the good has rightly been declared to be that at which all things aim.*
>
> **Aristotle**

Clarity—Eighty percent of success comes from being clear on who you are, what you believe in, and what you want. People with clarity keep their eyes transfixed on the goal.

> *I experience a period of frightening clarity in those moments when nature is so beautiful. I am no longer sure of myself, and the paintings appear as in a dream.*
>
> **Vincent Van Gough**

Confidence—Success comes to those who have the confidence to try, and the ability and dedication to keep trying till they win. Confidence is something that you cultivate, through affirmations and successful goal setting and attainment. Every success that you acquire, regardless of the size, will grow in your mind and heart. Each passing victory that you achieve builds more and more confidence in yourself. The next time you go to battle on your journey to success, this confidence will give you the power to draw from. Spend "5 minutes" a day to build confidence inside of yourself so you will be able to dip deeply into that well when you need it!

> *You have to expect things of yourself before you can do them.*
>
> **Michael Jordan**

Consistency—People that are successful understand that success does not follow the path of least resistance. Successful people follow a formula. I have found the 3 Ps—Passion, Purpose, and Perseverance—to be my formula. Rocky had passion and purpose, and he never gave up.

Sticking to doing the right things all the time will create your destiny. They consistently do the things that will bring them their success.

Consistency is the foundation of virtue.

Francis Bacon

Courage—This is one quality we need to succeed, it's often one of the qualities most in demand and least in supply, courage is the willingness to do the things you know are right, regardless of the consequences. Leaders are brave people. They know that even success has its challenges, yet they face them head on and move forward consistently, with clarity and confidence toward their goals.

Courage is being afraid but going on anyhow.

Dan Rather

The key is once you set sail on the Seven "Cs", you must stay true to your course. No matter how rocky the "Cs" may get, you must never give up. Here is a poem (author unknown) to hang on your cabin door, read it daily as you cruise the Seven "Cs."

Don't Quit

When things go wrong, as they sometimes will,
When the road you're trudging seems all uphill,
When the funds are low and the debts are high,
And you want to smile but you have to sigh,
When care is pressing you down a bit—
Rest if you must, but don't you quit.
Life is odd with its twists and turns,
As everyone sometimes learns.
And many a person turns about

When an individual might have won had he or she stuck it out.
Don't give up though the pace seems slow—
You may succeed with yet another blow.
Often the goal is nearer than it seems
To a faint and faltering woman or man;
Often the struggler has given up
When he or she might have captured the victor's cup;
And one learned too late when the night came down,
How close he or she was to the golden crown.
Success is failure turned inside out—
The silver tint of the clouds of doubt,
And when you never can tell how close you are,
It may be near when it seems afar;
So stick to the fight when you're hardest hit—
It's when things seem worst, you mustn't quit.

Imagine spending "5 minutes" a day caring for others, having confidence in yourself and the courage to do what needs to be done, and the clarity of purpose to keep your eye on your goals. To do this you will have to make good choices daily, the right choices. Begin by being consistent with your affirmations and your goal setting for "5 minutes" every day. By doing this you will develop such a strong character that people will follow and you will lead. As you navigate the Seven "Cs," there is much to learn and much to remember.

Now that you have sailed the Seven "Cs," you have learned there are many talents we need to master, to captain our own vessel. Once you master the Seven "Cs" you can unlock the treasures of success that are hidden in all of us. However you will need the keys to unlock these treasures. Here are my keys to a happy successful life:

"5 Minute" Keys to a Happy Life

1. Compliment 5 people everyday.

2. Watch a sunrise.

3. Watch a sunset.

4. Be the first to say "Hello."

5. Live beneath your means.

6. Forget the Joneses.

7. Smile even if your having a bad day.

8. Treat everyone as you want to be treated.

9. Be nice to everyone.

10. Make people feel good about themselves.

11. Never give up on anything; miracles happen, I'm living proof.

12. Try to remember someone new's name.

13. Pray not for things, but for wisdom and courage.

14. Be tough-minded, but tender-hearted.

15. Remember that overnight success usually takes 10 to 20 years and 7,000 hours of practice.

16. Try to leave everything better than you found it.

17. Remember that winners do what losers don't want to do.

18. When you arrive at your job in the morning, let the first thing you say brighten everyone's day.

19. Don't rain on other people's parades, shine on them.

20. Don't waste an opportunity to tell someone you love them.

21. If you want to lead the band, you have to face the music.

Now you have the 21 keys to the treasures of life. To access your treasures you must utilize these keys. Spend "5 minutes" each day over the next 21 days mastering each and everyone of the keys and watch it unlock your future success.

Most of the important things in the world have been accomplished by people who have kept on trying when there seemed to be no hope at all.

Dale Carnegie

Chapter 5

Personal Power

It takes "5 minutes" a day to close your eyes, review a chapter, a story, or your goals, and realize that we have three levels of consciousness. A conscious that acknowledges everything around us; a subconscious that, with our pre-programmed consciousness, coordinates things we do; and a super-conscious that can unlock the key elements of health and prosperity. The super-conscious can help us create what no one else has created. Many wise men and women have discovered the answers to the secret of life, while others look for a mystic to lead them to health, happiness, and wealth. Examples are the numerous infomercials, motivational books, tapes, DVDs, seminars, and speakers that are available to teach us how to tap into this power. The secret of the ages, the key to health and prosperity, has been found; all of these master motivators merely help you realize that you have the ability to change, that you are not shackled to your current situation, that your beliefs are what you believe in.

We are all products of nature. Think of yourself as no different than a caterpillar—break forth and fly as a butterfly. Once you believe, once you have faith, you are free to follow your dreams and find your destiny. To some, *The Secret* is a best-selling book; to others it's nothing more than an understanding of belief. "I AM" is a belief system that each of us can tap into. Personal greatness and achievements afford us the power to overcome any obstacle, but obstacles are what make life an adventure. By using your super-conscious mind, the world is your oyster. Many of the world's greatest thinkers have identified this power and presented a name for it. Ralph Waldo Emerson called it oversoul. He said, *"We lie in the lap of an immense intelligence that responds to our every need."* Napoleon Hill referred to this power as *"an infinite intelligence."* He claimed that the ability to access this intelligence was the key to the wealthy men and women he had researched over the years. D. D. Palmer and B. J. Palmer, the founders of chiropractic, recognized this power as innate intelligence, a universal intelligence. We must now tap into the power that lies within us to achieve what we want, what we need, what we are entitled to. The super-conscious mind is our infinite source of creativity. All truly classical art, music, and literature comes from people who have tapped into this creative power. We start to use our super-conscious mind when we dream and set goals, when we turn the invisible into the visible. Although through our education we have come to acknowledge a traditional direct approach, many of us have yet to fully believe or understand the infinite reservoir of power we harbor or how to fully utilize this power. Why something so simple appears so complex is baffling. Yet the Emersons, Edisons, Mozarts, Bachs, Beethovens, and Disneys all came to master this principle and we can, too.

A young man once went to Socrates and asked him how he could gain success. Socrates replied, *"Come with me."*

They walked together into a nearby lake, and when the water was about four feet deep, Socrates suddenly grabbed the young man and pushed his head into the water and held it there. Thinking it a joke, the young man did not resist. But as he was held under the water longer and longer, he became frantic. He struggled desperately to get free as his lungs burned from lack of oxygen. In one instant, he gathered all of his resources, reached into his super-conscious mind, and pooled all of his conscious and subconscious resources. With this tremendous effort, he twisted and turned and broke his way free. Coughing and sputtering for air, he demanded of Socrates why he had done such a thing.

Socrates replied, *"When you desire success with the same intensity that you desire to breathe, then nothing will stop you from getting it."*

When you desire success on a personal and professional level as much you desire air when you are submerged, this is when you will master your super-conscious. When you realize that you need whatever it is you need to survive, you will find a way to get it.

Socrates knew that all of the answers of the universe sit within. To win or lose, to survive or fail is choice. Failure is your choice, not your destiny. Within each and every one of us lies all the answers. Successes, health, happiness, all are within our grasp. Reach for them, fight for them. Today, let's take responsibility for our yesterday, and from this let us plan for our tomorrow. If it is to be, it is up to me. Take control of your life and your destiny, or your destiny will control you. Most often, we have only one boundary and one obstacle: ourselves.

Oliver Wendell Holmes said, *"A mind stretched by a new idea will never return to its original dimension."* Expand your vision; it's time to grow. Spend "5 minutes" today, just 300 seconds, dreaming of the person you want to be. Set a plan to be that person. Affirm the choice that you have made and take an actual step to become the person of your dreams.

Socrates knew the desire needed to be successful, but where do you learn the philosophies of success. Very few authors have had the influence of Dale Carnegie. He was born in 1888 in Missouri and was educated at Warrensburg State Teachers College. As a salesman and aspiring actor, he traveled to New York and began teaching communications classes to adults at the YMCA. In 1912, the world-famous Dale Carnegie Course® was born.

He authored several bestsellers, including *How To Win Friends and Influence People.* Over 50 million copies of Mr. Carnegie's books have been printed and published in 38 languages.

Mr. Carnegie was a prominent lecturer of his day and a sought-after counselor to world leaders. Dale Carnegie founded what is today a worldwide network of over 3,000 instructors and offices in more than 70 countries. Let me share with you his Golden Rules. Please spend the next "5 minutes" reading them and the rest of your life implementing them.

"5 Minute" Principles from How to Win Friends and Influence People

Spend "5 Minutes" a Day to Become a Friendlier Person

1. Don't criticize, condemn, or complain.

2. Give honest, sincere appreciation.

3. Arouse in the other person an eager want.

4. Become genuinely interested in other people.

5. Smile.

6. Remember that a person's name is to that person the sweetest and most important sound in any language.

7. Be a good listener. Encourage others to talk about themselves.

8. Talk in terms of another person's interests.

9. Make the other person feel important—and do it sincerely.

Spend "5 Minutes" a Day to Win People to Your Way of Thinking

1. The only way to get the best of an argument is to avoid it.

2. Show respect for the other person's opinion. Never say, "you're wrong."

3. If you are wrong, admit it quickly and emphatically.

4. Begin in a friendly way.

5. Get the other person saying, "yes, yes" immediately.

6. Let the other person do a great deal of the talking.

7. Try honestly to see things from the other person's point of view.

8. Be sympathetic with the other person's ideas and desires.

9. Appeal to the nobler motives.

10. Dramatize your ideas.

11. Throw down a challenge.

Spend "5 Minutes" a Day to Be a Leader

1. Begin with praise and honest appreciation.

2. Call attention to people's mistakes indirectly.

3. Talk about your own mistakes before criticizing the other person.

4. Ask questions instead of giving direct orders.

5. Let the other person save face.

6. Praise the slightest improvement and praise every improvement. Be "hearty in your approbation and lavish in your praise."

7. Give the other person a fine reputation to live up to.

8. Use encouragement. Make the fault seem easy to correct.

9. Make the other person happy about doing the thing you suggest.

"5 Minute" Principles from How to Stop Worrying and Start Living

Spend "5 Minutes" a Day Overcoming Worry

1. Live in "day-tight compartments."

2. How to face trouble:
    Ask yourself, "What is the worst that can possibly happen?"
    Prepare to accept the worst.
    Try to improve on the worst.

3. Remind yourself of the exorbitant price you can pay for worry in terms of your health.

Spend "5 Minutes" a Day Analyzing Worry

1. Get all the facts.

2. Weigh all the facts—then come to a decision.

3. Once a decision is reached—act!

4. Write out and answer the following questions:
    What is the problem?
    What are the causes of the problem?
    What are the possible solutions?
    What is the best possible solution?

Spend "5 Minutes" a Day Breaking the Worry Habit Before It Breaks You

1. Keep busy.

2. Don't fuss about trifles.

3. Use the law of averages to outlaw your worries.

4. Cooperate with the inevitable.

5. Decide just how much anxiety a thing may be worth and refuse to give it more.

6. Don't worry about the past.

Spend "5 Minutes" a Day to Cultivate a Mental Attitude that will Bring You Peace and Happiness

1. Fill your mind with thoughts of peace, courage, health, and hope.

2. Never try to get even with your enemies.

3. Expect ingratitude.

4. Count your blessings—not your troubles.

5. Do not imitate others.

6. Try to profit from your losses.

7. Create happiness for others.

The Perfect Way to Conquer Worry

1. Pray for "5 minutes" every day.

Spend "5 Minutes" a Day to Not Worry about Criticism

1. Remember that unjust criticism is often a disguised compliment.

2. Do the very best you can.

3. Analyze your own mistakes and criticize yourself.

4. Prevent Fatigue and Worry and Keep Your Energy and Spirits High

5. Rest before you get tired.

6. Learn to relax at your work.

7. Protect your health and appearance by relaxing at home.

8. Apply these four good working habits:
    Clear your desk of all papers except those relating to the immediate problem at hand.
    Do things in the order of their importance.
    When you face a problem, solve it then and there if you have the facts necessary to make a decision.
    Learn to organize, deputize, and supervise.

9. Put enthusiasm into your work.

10. Don't worry about insomnia.

Wow, as you can see, there is a reason why over 50 million copies of Dale Carnegie's books have been sold. He offers us simple rules to live by. Study them for "5 minutes" each day so that you can change yourself, your life, and your relationships. Allow yourself to succeed and conquer all your fears. Meditate and discover yourself, your strengths, and your mission and purpose in life. This is a small investment for a large return. Follow these rules and you will never again feel alone.

None of us in life are alone when it comes to facing problems. The key is to face them. *"If you want to lead the band, you have to face the music."* From this day forth, choose to succeed in life. If things don't go your way, then fight your way back.

My wife and I chose to get our lives back, to walk again, to talk again, to love again, to eat again, to open our eyes again, and to breathe on our own again. What was once so simple to do, so simple for so many of us, was considered a miracle. We take so much of life for granted. The miracles in life are life itself. To walk, to talk, to see, and to hear. It's our ability to think, to communicate, to set goals, to love and care, that sets us apart from the animal kingdom. We are so consumed with material things that we forget what is really material.

Let's take "5 minutes" now to give thanks for all the good in life we have. God has blessed each of us with life; our blessing to God is what we do with our life.

Choose to live, to laugh, to love, and to learn. The only thing I can promise you about life, is you will not get out of it alive, so live each day as if it's your last and learn to cherish the moment.

A man who dares to waste one hour of time has not discovered the value of life.

Charles Darwin

Chapter 6

Be a "Liver" of Life or You'll End Up a Gallbladder

One day, the devil decided to have a garage sale. In this sale he wanted to include his magnificent set of tools, such as fear, anxiety, depression, procrastination, negativity, hostility, and jealousy. As one of his demons helped him lay out these items for his sale, he noticed off in the corner an old wedge that boasted the most expensive price tag of all. The demon asked the devil why such an old, rusted wedge was displayed proudly with the most expensive of his tools. The devil responded, *"This is my most valuable tool, the Wedge of Discouragement. When I use this wedge, I am able to pry my way into the subconscious of men and women. Once discouragement sets in, all of the other tools automatically do their work."*

Do not let anyone steal your dreams or visions. Be a liver (of life) not a gallbladder. Life is a combination lock; a lock filled with numbers. We must turn these numbers in the right sequence, in the right direction, to unlock the treasures within. We all know our combination; we just don't always follow the right direction, or move in the right sequence. Success, health, and happiness are not miracles. The only real miracle is life. Success does not depend on luck; it counts on effort. It does not matter who you are, as long as you follow the combination to success.

Applying this metaphor to everyday life, you could say that there is

38

a combination of thoughts and actions that will enable you to accomplish whatever you want through your super-consciousness. We have the ability to unlock the potential that lies in each of us. You will find the combination if you search for it. Health, wealth, happiness, success, and peace of mind are inherent within each of us. If you do the right things, in the right manner, at the right time, you will get the right results. Successful people do what unsuccessful people dare not to do—or do not even want to do. Yet every success we have is based on some degree of failure.

We were not born walking and talking. The first time we walked, we fell. The first words we uttered, we stuttered. The first time we read, added, multiplied, divided, shot a basket, or swung a bat or a golf club, we met with some degree of failure. Yet, we persisted. Remember how awkward your first date was? I'll bet it wasn't your last date. Life is a culmination of learning experiences based entirely on obstacles and failures. Remember, it's the rocks in the stream that give the river its music.

There was once a little boy who armed himself with a bat and ball and went out to play. He began by throwing the ball up in the air and trying to hit it as it came down. However, with every toss came a strike. Time and time again he threw the ball in the air attempting to hit it. After an hour of futility, the boy picked up the ball and said, *"Boy, am I a good pitcher."*

Now is the time for achievement. Never before in the history of the world have more people had so many accomplishments.

Dennis Whatley said, *"Failure is only a temporary change in direction to set you straight for your next success."*

Through the course of life, I have formulated 5 basic principles:

1. Life is difficult. It always has been and always will be.

2. Everything "I am" to be is up to me.

3. You can learn anything you need to learn, become anyone you want to become, achieve anything you want to achieve.

4. Life has few limitations, and most of those are on the inside, not the outside.

5. The sky is not the limit; the sky is only as far as we can see. The universe is infinite, and so we have no limits.

Recently the world was saddened by the loss of innovator, motivator, entrepreneur and genius Steve Jobs, at the tender young age of 56. With all his talent, all his money, the one thing he could not buy was time. You'll learn, however, that he lived his life for the moment and invested his time on this planet wisely. This story was sent to me by my great friend Bill Meyer; it moved me as I'm sure it will move you. Steve Jobs was a man who embraced the difficulties of life, who knew there were no limits, who visualized the impossible and made it possible. This is the "Stay Hungry. Stay Foolish" address delivered by Steve Jobs in 2005 at Stanford University.

> I am honored to be with you today at your commencement from one of the finest universities in the world. I never graduated from college. Truth be told, this is the closest I've ever gotten to a college graduation. Today, I want to tell you three stories from my life. That's it. No big deal. Just three stories.
>
> The first story is about connecting the dots. I dropped out of Reed College after the first six months, but then stayed around as a drop-in for another 18 months or so before I really quit. So why did I drop out?
>
> It started before I was born. My biological mother was a young, unwed college graduate student, and she decided to put me up for adoption. She felt very strongly that I should be adopted by college graduates, so everything was all set for me to be adopted at birth by a lawyer and his wife. Except that when I popped out they decided at the last minute that they really wanted a girl. So my parents, who were on a

waiting list, got a call in the middle of the night asking: "We have an unexpected baby boy; do you want him?" They said: "Of course." My biological mother later found out that my mother had never graduated from college and that my father had never graduated from high school. She refused to sign the final adoption papers. She only relented a few months later when my parents promised that I would someday go to college.

And 17 years later I did go to college. But I naively chose a college that was almost as expensive as Stanford, and all of my working-class parents' savings were being spent on my college tuition. After six months, I couldn't see the value in it. I had no idea what I wanted to do with my life and no idea how college was going to help me figure it out. And here I was spending all of the money my parents had saved their entire life. So I decided to drop out and trust that it would all work out okay. It was pretty scary at the time, but looking back it was one of the best decisions I ever made. The minute I dropped out I could stop taking the required classes that didn't interest me and begin dropping in on the ones that looked interesting.

It wasn't all romantic. I didn't have a dorm room, so I slept on the floor in friends' rooms, I returned Coke bottles for the 5¢ deposits to buy food with, and I would walk the 7 miles across town every Sunday night to get one good meal a week at the Hare Krishna temple. I loved it. And much of what I stumbled into by following my curiosity and intuition turned out to be priceless later on. Let me give you one example.

Reed College at that time offered perhaps the best calligraphy instruction in the country. Throughout the campus every poster, every label on every drawer, was beautifully hand calligraphed. Because I had dropped out and didn't have to take the normal classes, I decided to take a calligraphy class

41

to learn how to do this. I learned about serif and san serif typefaces, about varying the amount of space between different letter combinations, about what makes great typography great. It was beautiful, historical, artistically subtle in a way that science can't capture, and I found it fascinating.

None of this had even a hope of any practical application in my life. But ten years later, when we were designing the first Macintosh computer, it all came back to me. And we designed it all into the Mac. It was the first computer with beautiful typography. If I had never dropped in on that single course in college, the Mac would have never had multiple typefaces or proportionally spaced fonts. And since Windows just copied the Mac, it's likely that no personal computer would have them. If I had never dropped out, I would have never dropped in on this calligraphy class, and personal computers might not have the wonderful typography that they do. Of course, it was impossible to connect the dots looking forward when I was in college. But it was very, very clear looking backwards ten years later.

Again, you can't connect the dots looking forward; you can only connect them looking backwards. So you have to trust that the dots will somehow connect in your future. You have to trust in something—your gut, destiny, life, karma, whatever. This approach has never let me down, and it has made all the difference in my life.

My second story is about love and loss. I was lucky—I found what I loved to do early in life. Woz and I started Apple in my parents garage when I was 20. We worked hard, and in 10 years Apple had grown from just the two of us in a garage into a $2 billion company with over 4,000 employees. We had just released our finest creation—the Macintosh—a year earlier, and I had just turned 30. And then I got fired. How can you get fired from a company you started? Well, as Apple grew we hired someone who I thought was very talented to run the company with me, and for the first year or so things went well. But then our visions of the future began to diverge and eventually we had a falling out. When we did, our Board of Directors sided with him. So at 30 I was out. And very publicly out. What had been the focus of my entire adult life was gone, and it was devastating.

I really didn't know what to do for a few months. I felt that I had let the previous generation of entrepreneurs down—that I had dropped the baton as it was being passed to me. I met with David Packard and Bob Noyce and tried to apologize for screwing up so badly. I was a very public failure, and I even thought about running away from the valley. But something slowly began to dawn on me—I still loved what I did. The turn of events at Apple had not changed that one bit. I had been rejected, but I was still in love. And so I decided to start over.

I didn't see it then, but it turned out that getting fired from Apple was the best thing that could have ever happened to me. The heaviness of being successful was replaced by the lightness of being a beginner again, less sure about everything. It freed me to enter one of the most creative periods of my life.

During the next five years, I started a company named NeXT, another company named Pixar, and fell in love with an amazing woman who would become my wife. Pixar went on to create the world's first computer animated feature film, Toy Story, and is now the most successful animation studio in the world. In a remarkable turn of events, Apple bought NeXT, I returned to Apple, and the technology we developed at NeXT is at the heart of Apple's current renaissance. And Laurene and I have a wonderful family together.

I'm pretty sure none of this would have happened if I hadn't been fired from Apple. It was awful tasting medicine, but I guess the patient needed it. Sometimes life hits you in the head with a brick. Don't lose faith. I'm convinced that the only thing that kept me going was that I loved what I did. You've got to find what you love. And that is as true for your work as it is for your lovers. Your work is going to fill a large part of your life, and the only way to be truly satisfied is to do what you believe is great work. And the only way to do great work is to love what you do. If you haven't found it yet, keep looking. Don't settle. As with all matters of the heart, you'll know when you find it. And, like any great relationship, it just gets better and better as the years roll on. So keep looking until you find it. Don't settle.

My third story is about death. When I was 17, I read a quote that went something like, "If you live each day as if it was your last, someday you'll most certainly be right." It made an impression on me, and since then, for the past 33 years, I have looked in the mirror every morning and asked myself, "If today were the last day of my life, would I want to do what I am about to do today?" And whenever the answer has been "No" for too many days in a row, I know I need to change something.

Remembering that I'll be dead soon is the most important tool I've ever encountered to help me make the big choices in life. Because almost everything—all external expectations, all pride, all fear of embarrassment or failure—these things just fall away in the face of death, leaving only what is truly important. Remembering that you are going to die is the best way I know to avoid the trap of thinking you have something to lose. You are already naked. There is no reason not to follow your heart.

About a year ago I was diagnosed with cancer. I had a scan

at 7:30 in the morning, and it clearly showed a tumor on my pancreas. I didn't even know what a pancreas was. The doctors told me this was almost certainly a type of cancer that is incurable, and that I should expect to live no longer than three to six months. My doctor advised me to go home and get my affairs in order, which is doctor's code for prepare to die. It means to try to tell your kids everything you thought you'd have the next 10 years to tell them in just a few months. It means to make sure everything is buttoned up so that it will be as easy as possible for your family. It means to say your goodbyes.

I lived with that diagnosis all day. Later that evening I had a biopsy, where they stuck an endoscope down my throat, through my stomach and into my intestines, put a needle into my pancreas, and got a few cells from the tumor. I was sedated, but my wife, who was there, told me that when they viewed the cells under a microscope the doctors started crying because it turned out to be a very rare form of pancreatic cancer that is curable with surgery. I had the surgery and I'm fine now.

This was the closest I've been to facing death, and I hope it's the closest I get for a few more decades. Having lived through it, I can now say this to you with a bit more certainty than when death was a useful but purely intellectual concept: No one wants to die. Even people who want to go to heaven don't want to die to get there. And yet death is the destination we all share. No one has ever escaped it. And that is as it should be, because Death is very likely the single best invention of Life. It is Life's change agent. It clears out the old to make way for the new. Right now the new is you, but someday not too long from now, you will gradually become the old and be cleared away. Sorry to be so dramatic, but it is quite true.

Your time is limited, so don't waste it living someone else's life. Don't be trapped by dogma—which is living with the results of other people's thinking. Don't let the noise of others' opinions drown out your own inner voice. And most important, have the courage to follow your heart and intuition. They somehow already know what you truly want to become. Everything else is secondary.

When I was young, there was an amazing publication called The Whole Earth Catalog, which was one of the bibles of my generation. It was created by a fellow named Stewart Brand not far from here in Menlo Park, and he brought it to life with his poetic touch. This was in the late 1960s, before personal computers and desktop publishing, so it was all made with typewriters, scissors, and polaroid cameras. It was sort of like Google in paperback form, 35 years before Google came along: it was idealistic, and overflowing with neat tools and great notions.

Stewart and his team put out several issues of The Whole Earth Catalog, and then when it had run its course, they put out a final issue. It was the mid-1970s, and I was your age. On the back cover of their final issue was a photograph of an early morning country road, the kind you might find yourself hitchhiking on if you were so adventurous. Beneath it were the words, "Stay Hungry. Stay Foolish." It was their farewell message as they signed off. Stay Hungry. Stay Foolish. And I have always wished that for myself. And now, as you graduate to begin anew, I wish that for you.

Stay Hungry. Stay Foolish.

Thank you all very much.

If necessity is the mother of invention, then experience is the father of learning. Let us be livers of life, not gallbladders. Do not let life's bile interrupt your quest for success. The difference between a .300 hitter and a .200 hitter is only one hit every ten times at bat. But the difference in salary is probably a million dollars a year! It's my belief that any .200 hitter could be a .300 hitter. He could increase his speed and spend more time in the batter's box. Remember—only one hit every ten times at bat.

Recognize that the key to life is within you. We must acquire the building blocks of our, spirit step by step, one block at a time. The first building block from which we may shape a positive mental attitude is the habit of moving within definitions of purpose (in planning our life and living our plan). We must move in the direction of our goals, of our dreams. If we don't know what we want from life, it's time we define just what it is will make our lives complete. Without a purpose, without comprehensive plans for the fulfillment of whatever goals we set, our mind is vulnerable to negative and lazy attitudes. Set the plan and be relentless in its pursuit.

Roger Bannister had a goal that for thousands of years no man had accomplished. His goal was to run a three-minute mile: one mile in less than four minutes. No one had ever run a mile in under four minutes. While Bannister's relentless pursuit of his dream contributed to his success in accomplishing his goal, the story does not end there.

For centuries, man was on this quest to run a mile in under four minutes. Doctors and scientists said it physically could not be done. But within one year after Roger Bannister accomplished the feat, three other runners also broke the four-minute barrier. You see, once people accept the intangible possibilities as realities, goals become easier to accomplish.

A little boy went into a drug store, reached for a soda carton, and pulled it over to the telephone (obviously, this was before the days of cell phones). He climbed onto the carton so that he could reach the buttons on the phone and proceeded to punch in the seven digits. I listened to the following conversation:

He said, *"Lady, I want to cut your lawn."*

The woman replied, *"I already have someone to cut my lawn."*

The boy responded, *"Lady, I'll cut your lawn for half the price of the person who cuts your lawn, now."*

The woman responded that she was very satisfied with the person who was presently cutting her lawn.

The little boy found yet more perseverance and offered, *"Lady, I'll even sweep your curb and sidewalk, so on Sunday you'll have the prettiest lawn in all of North Palm Beach, Florida."*

Again the woman answered in the negative.

With a smile on his face, the little boy replaced the receiver.

The owner of the store walked over to the boy and said, *"Son, I like your attitude, I like your positive spirit. Son, I'd like to offer you a job."*

The little boy replied, **"No thanks. I was checking on the job I already have."**

It's not likely someone with that spirit or attitude will end up on any employment line. Are you doing the best job in life or in business you can? If not, why not?

If the wedge of discouragement is the Devils tool, then affirmations are God's tool. Affirmations are positive sayings that lead to positive thoughts that lead to positive actions. Affirm yourself today, set a goal today, to give more, to be more, to be the best you can be. Take "5 minutes" right here, right now and state your daily affirmation. Here is mine:

I am happy, I am healthy, I am successful. God has blessed me with the gift of life and I will not take this gift for granted. My body is functioning at 100 percent, 100 percent of the time. My body is breaking down fat and turning the food that I eat into muscle. I utilize the elements—the sun, the air, and the water—and these elements revitalize my body. They increase my life energy and guide my body to a happier, healthier existence. I am free of stress. I do not allow stress into my consciousness. I am relaxed mentally and physically. I am mentally and physically prepared to enter this day to succeed. I am prepared for the obstacles and challenges that life has to offer me. I turn any and all obstacles and challenges into my successes. From these successes I increase my strength and confidence. I acknowledge that the world is filled with abundance. An abundance of wealth, health, and happiness. I am part of this abundance. Today, I think only good thoughts. I say only nice things. I do only good deeds. I eat only good foods. I do not allow negative sources to enter my body. I reward my body for rewarding me with life. Today, I am happy, I am healthy, I am terrific. Today, I am successful. Today, I love and am loved. Today my life is filled with abundance. To learn how you can have health *and* wealth, go to www.5minutemotivator.com.

Now is our time to love, laugh, and learn. Many of us have been suppressed or oppressed by the limitations of others. We have not opened up the boundaries within. Let's take our "5 minutes" every day to open our hearts, our minds, and our souls to ensnare our visions. There is no better time than now, and no better day than today. Stay Hungry. Stay Foolish.

*A successful man is one who can lay a firm foundation with
the bricks others have thrown at him.*

David Brinkley

Chapter 7

The Robbers of Success

This story that I first read in the book, *Think and Grow Rich* by
Napoleon Hill, concerns one R.U. Darby who went West to make his
fortune during the Gold Rush days. After weeks of labor, he was rewarded
by the glitter of golden ore. Realizing the need for proper machinery,
Darby went to his friends and family to raise money for the necessary
equipment. Once he completed this task, he went back to the mines,
now with proper equipment and a crew. The first car of golden ore was
mined and shipped, and the return proved they had one of the richest
mines in Colorado. Only a few more cars of ore were needed to clear of
Darby's debts; then it would be pure profit.

However, as in life, success is not always easy. When they went
back into the mine they came up empty; the vein of gold had apparently
disappeared. The miners desperately tried to pick up the vein again. After
several failures over many months, they conceded their defeat. Darby
was influenced by the opinions of the other miners that the vein was now
long gone and it was time to move on. Being an honest and honorable
man he sold all the machinery to pay the remainder of his debts.

The junk man however was curious of Darby's success, so upon
acquiring the machinery and the mine, he hired an independent engineer
for a second opinion. Well, you guessed it, the engineer advised the new
owner that Darby had failed because the miners were not familiar with

fault lines. The engineer then guided him to a spot just *three feet* from where Darby's men had stopped drilling and that is precisely where the gold was found. The junk man mined millions of dollars in gold ore because he knew enough to take one more step before giving up.

When robbed of their dreams, many a man would have quit and given up. But Darby's story has a happy ending, for he learned a lesson more valuable then gold. He never forgot that he lost a fortune because he stopped three feet too soon. As an insurance salesman, he vowed never to give up because he was told "no" by a prospective customer. Darby went on to become one of a select group who sold over a million dollars worth of life insurance annually at a time when a million was a million and a difficult feat to attain. He learned never to let anyone rob him of his dreams or to give up, regardless of the price.

What robs so many of us from our dreams is often nothing more than negative thoughts. Negative thoughts are the robbers of success. Negative emotions are the robbers of the emotions of life. They are the cause of sickness and disease, the root of both underachievement and failure. They are carriers of all illness. They make the physically fit—physically ill, the happy—unhappy, the certain—uncertain, the strong—weak, the content—discontent, and the tall—small. Negative emotions are parasites. They steal the joy a person might feel from achievement. They are enemies of happiness. A positive attitude and mindset is the antidote for negative emotions. The elimination of negative emotions is the key for anyone who aspires to great success and achievement.

W. Clement Stone said, *"There is little difference among people, but that little difference makes a big difference. The little difference is attitude; the big difference is whether it's positive or negative."*

Peace of mind is the pinnacle of human existence. Peace of mind can only exist in the absence of negative emotions. This concept is no different than the fact that you cannot smile and frown at the same time; you cannot host positive and negative simultaneously. On my quest for the secret of life, I realized that all of the problems of life, in one form or another, are rooted in negative emotion. It became clear to me that the elimination of negative emotions would make life wonderful, a world of peace. It's amazing that we sit in the sanctuaries of our homes or offices while we have a world at war, a world in crisis. The problems in the Middle East, Sarajevo, Rwanda, Haiti, and other parts of the globe are rooted in generations of negative emotions. We know this unrest only as images on the television screen, not the cold, hard reality that confronts the people of those ravaged lands on a daily basis. They put their lives on the line for causes that must seem utterly hopeless. We remain in the comfort of our offices and our homes with far less significant problems, yet we act as if all the troubles of the world are ours. Wayne Dyer said that life consists of two types of people: eagles and ducks. Ducks quack incessantly about the slightest problem. *"Why me? Quack, quack. Life is not fair, quack, quack. I could have been a contender, quack, quack."*

Eagles, on the other hand, do not have time to quack, as they soar majestically through the heavens as an everlasting symbol of freedom. Each of us must decide: *"Am I a duck or an eagle?"*

So many of us have the eyesight of an eagle, yet we are constrained by having the vision of a clam. We were not born with negative emotions; we acquired them. They changed the natural into the unnatural. Our life is a reflection of our attitudes. A new attitude will invariably create a new result.

Within each of us we have two dogs: a red dog that represents negative emotions, and a white dog that represents positive emotions. Throughout our days, these dogs fight for control over our thinking. Remember, the dog you feed the most will ultimately become the stronger dog, the dominant dog. To beat the red dog, i.e., negative dog, you must starve it. Let the white dog build his strength and dominate your emotions. Every hour of every day you must feed that white dog. Because at the end of the day, your emotions will hang in the balance between the two dogs and which dog you fed the most.

Accept responsibility for who you are, where you are, what you are, and what you have. Once you have begun to accept responsibility for every part of your life, encourage your friends, family, and associates to do the same thing. The ultimate key to inner peace and outer success is contained within yourself and your response to the world around you. The universal law states that everything you are today is the result of your habitual way of thinking. The law of correspondence states that your outer world is a physical manifestation of your inner world. Everything you are you have learned, and anything learned can be unlearned. You hold the key to the lock on your attitudes, habits, and emotions. The Bible states, *"You will be renewed by renewing your mind."*

In life we can be a winner or a loser, a victor or a victim, a winner or a whiner. A "liver" or a "gallbladder."

Victor language consists of phrases like, *"I can,"* and victim language consists of phrases like, *"I can't."* If you went to a doctor and he said, *"I'll try to help you,"* you might seriously consider getting a second opinion.

The word *"try"* is victim language, as in *"I can't," "I have to," "I'll try," "I wish," "I'm sorry," "don't blame me,"* or *"that's not my fault."*

By utilizing these words, you are fueling the red dog, allowing him to dominate and intimidate your subconscious. Make the decision now to be a victor, not a victim. When you remove victim language from your vocabulary, speak with definition and conviction.

Feed the white dog by saying, *"I will"* or *"I won't."* You control your destiny.

Say "I want to," rather than *"I have to."*

And lastly, but most importantly, say, *"I can"* or *"I will"* instead of *"I can't"* or *"I wish."*

Be definite in thought and purpose or, as Yogi Berra once said, *"If you don't know where you're going, you'll probably end up someplace else."*

Be a can-do kind of person; be a dreamer and don't let anyone or anything rob you of your dreams, especially not yourself. ***Spend "5 minutes" a day developing winning habits and feeding the white dog.***

Winners

Winners develop the habit of doing the things
that losers don't like to do.

We first make our habits, and then our habits make us.

The "5 Minute" Habits of a Winner

1. Don't condemn, criticize, or complain. Think of ways
   to improve the situation. The big rewards are paid for
   finding the solution, not the difficulty.

2. Show real, honest, and hearty appreciation. Let others
   know they're loved.

3. Think good thoughts about other people—and yourself.

4. Give before you get. Always give others a reason to agree
   with you before asking anything of them. (If there were a
   way that *you…*)

5. Smile often—it generates enthusiasm, friendliness, and
   goodwill.

6. Remember names. A person's name is the sweetest, most
   important sound he hears and instantly captures his
   attention every time it's used.

7. Be an effective communicator by listening. Encourage
   others to talk about themselves by asking questions.
   (When, Where, Who, What, How, *Why?*)

8. Think, Act, and Look happy and successful and you
   will begin to think, feel, and actually become *happy* and
   successful.

9. Never engage in worry conversations or participate in gossip sessions.

10. Always greet others with a positive, cheerful statement, not the question, "How are you?"

11. Respond to another's question, "How are you?" with an enthusiastic, meaningful "*Terrific!*"

12. Look for and expect *good* things to happen to you… inquire of others: "What *good* things are happening with you today?"

Pick one rule at a time.

Practice it earnestly every day for at least "5 minutes" for a full week.

Change your thoughts and you change your world.
Norman Vincent Peale

In "5 minutes" a day we can alter our attitude. Let's spend the next "5 minutes" and "5 minutes" a day, from this day forth, feeding our white dog. Let's take control of our lives by feeding the right dog, the white dog. Is your white dog hungry? You bet it is. Feed your white dog today and every day for "5 minutes" and make it your strong dog, your dominant dog.

The difference between perseverance and obstinacy is that one comes from a strong will, and the other from a strong won't.

Henry Ward Beecher

Chapter 8

Mission Possible!

Good day, friend. Your mission, should you choose to accept it, is complex. It's your objective to combat the genocide of positive thinking and to create a happy, positive, philosophy of wellness in your community. In order to accomplish your objective, you must first develop and then read your mission statement. The physical and mental health of the world is at stake. This mission will affect the lives of your family, your children, grandchildren, and the world at large. In order to succeed, you must be willing to sacrifice whatever it takes. The information enclosed in this communiqué will assist you in devising a plan to derail the genocide of wellness.

This genocide is fed by pharmaceutical and advertising mediums. Billions of dollars are spent on depression medication—that fact alone is depressing. We could get out of our national debt by putting this money to health and happiness. Our adults are depressed and our children are obese and hyperactive. No wonder the world is laughing at us. We need to throw away the drugs and begin exercising our bodies and our minds. To prevent the further diffusion of these antigens, we must educate our families our friends our communities to the power of one, the power of self. One man overcame depression, overcame a nervous breakdown to lead our country to greatness. We must look for strength within, not just in a prescription bottle.

You've probably already learned (perhaps to your sorrow) that you are what you eat. But has it ever occurred to you that you are what you think? Just as a diet high in junk foods will distort your body, a mind full of junk thoughts will distort your goals, dreams, and ambitions.

We can only defeat the genocide of negative thinking with positive affirmations. We learned in Chapter 6 of the power of affirmations. I shared with you my daily affirmation in that chapter. Did you wake up "5 minutes" early today? If so, that is the best time to cite your affirmations. In review, an affirmation is a positive statement about yourself or your circumstances. Affirmations enable you to program yourself to succeed by removing fears or thoughts of failure that your subconscious has accumulated over the years. In many ways, the brain is like a computer; what you get out of it depends on what you put into it.

You can say affirmations aloud, repeat them silently to yourself, write them down, or even sing them! The more you repeat an affirmation, the greater power you give it, so repeat your affirmations frequently and with conviction. Believe me, you do have the time to do this. You can say your affirmations while in the shower, while you exercise, or on your way to work (instead of cursing traffic). Affirm as you cook dinner, vacuum the carpet, or mow your lawn.

Let me provide you with a couple of hints, to help you use affirmations to their best advantage. One, use them in the present tense. For example, *"I am slender and healthy,"* rather than *"I will be slender and healthy."* Two, use positive rather than negative language. For example, *"I live in harmony with my family,"* rather than, *"I no longer shout at my family."*

If you doubt the power of affirmations, take a look around you. Better yet, take a look inside yourself. Have you ever known a highly successful person who was riddled with doubts and insecurities? Much of who you are today is a reflection of who you think you are.

Muhammad Ali made his affirmation into legend. He wasn't born a great boxer. He trained, struggled, and dreamed of his triumph. And

57

through his rise to the championship of the world, he affirmed, *"I am the greatest!"* Even after he eventually lost, he didn't say, *"I was the greatest."* He said, *"I am still the greatest"* and went on to regain his title a record three times.

Successful people think successful thoughts. The genocide to success is bad thinking. Imagine legendary Dallas Cowboys coach Tom Landry who, during his first season with the Cowboys, didn't win a single game. His record was zero wins, eleven losses, and one tie. Yet he went on to become one of the most successful coaches in their franchise history. He never gave in to the media or the ridicule; he knew he was a winner and kept telling himself that, as well.

I encourage you to turn your personality into a success personality. Understand that the only psychology to success is the desire to succeed. You may be wondering what your personality has to do with your health. Many studies suggest that we can think our way to health—or illness. One such study conducted by John W. Shaffer and Pirkko L. Graves at Johns Hopkins University School of Medicine revealed that men who hide their feelings are much more likely to develop cancer than men who express their feelings. The researchers also found that loners were 16 times more likely to get cancer than emotionally expressive men.

Through affirmations, we can express our feelings, needs, and desires with confidence that they can be fulfilled:

"I am now at my optimum weight."
"I enjoy excellent health and limitless vitality."
"All of my relationships are loving and fulfilling."
"I love my work and always do an excellent job."

Let's look at Dr. Seuss's affirmation in regards to work.

I love my job, I love the pay
I love it more and more each day
I love my boss, he is the best
I love his boss and all the rest

I love my office and its location
I hate to have to go on vacation
I love my furniture, drab and grey
and piles of paper that grow each day!
I think my job is really swell,
there's nothing else I love so well.
I love to work among my peers,
I love their leers, and jeers, and sneers.
I love my computer and its software;
I hug it often though it won't care.
I love each program and every file.
I'd love them more if they worked a while.

I am happy to be here. I am. I am.
I'm the happiest slave of the Firm, I am.
I love this work, I love these chores.
I love the meetings with deadly bores.
I love my job - I'll say it again-
I even love those friendly men.
Those friendly men who've come today.
In clean white coats to take me away!!!

Feel free to make your own affirmations using the language that feels right for your particular situation and goals. You hold in your heart the key to the treasure of affirmations.

One of the main keys is just being happy with yourself. Stop worrying about what you don't have and start appreciating what you do have. Affirm your uniqueness regardless of your job, position, or station in life. It's your attitude, your love of life that is your greatest asset. Let me share a story with you.

One day an American investment banker was at the pier of a small coastal Mexican village when a small boat with just one fisherman docked one afternoon. Inside the small boat were several large yellowfin tuna. The American complimented the Mexican on the quality of his fish and asked how long it took to catch them.

The Mexican replied, *"Only a little while."*

The American then asked, *"Why didn't you stay out longer and catch more fish?"*

The Mexican said, *"Why, with this I have more than enough to support my family's needs."*

The American then asked, *"But what do you do during a normal day?"*

The Mexican fisherman said, *"I sleep late till about 10, have a little coffee with my wife, play with my children, then I go fish a little. Then I come home, clean my fish, and take siesta with my wife, Maria. When I awake, we stroll into the village each evening where I sip wine and play guitar with my amigos. I have a full and busy life."*

The American scoffed, *"I'm a Yale MBA and I'm positive I could change your life. You should spend more time fishing and with the proceeds buy a bigger boat: With the proceeds from the bigger boat you could buy several boats. Eventually you would have a fleet of fishing boats. Instead of selling your catch to a middleman you would sell directly to the processor; eventually opening your own cannery. You would control the product, processing and distribution. You will eventually need to leave this small coastal fishing village and move to Mexico City, then Florida and eventually New York where you will run your ever-expanding enterprise."*

The Mexican fisherman asked, *"But, how long will this all take?"*

To which the American replied, *"15 to 20 years."*

"But what then?" asked the Mexican.

The American smiled, laughed and said that's the best part. *"When the time is right you would announce an IPO and sell your company stock to the public and become very rich, you would make millions."*

"Millions?...Then what?"

The American said, *"Then you would retire. Move to a small coastal fishing village where you would sleep late, fish a little, play with your kids, take siesta with your wife, stroll to the village in the evenings where you could sip wine and play your guitar with your amigos."*

The Mexican smiled, shook his head and walked away.

Each and every one of us has so much, yet we always want so much more, forgetting that what we already have may be perfect. The knowledge of who we are, and what we will act as, is an antidote for any epidemic. This chapter will not self-destruct in 30 seconds, but its content, which will take only "5 minutes" to absorb, will weaken the enemy if it falls into their hands.

We must become the change we want to see in the world.

Ghandi

Chapter 9

Making the Difference

It's simple to say that we must always start at the beginning. Each day has a beginning and an end, as does each project, goal, story, attitude, etc. The beauty of new days is that they offer new beginnings. William James said, *"Believe that life is worth living and your belief will create the fact."* Let us forget yesterday, concentrate on today, and prepare for tomorrow.

Anthony Robbins said that goals have a beginning and an end; however, I believe a mission statement is infinite. A mission statement is the fuel of our very purpose, our very existence. A mission is more than a duty or a task. It's a dream, a vision, a purpose, which drives you. On June 22, 1989, President George Bush stood on the White House lawn and told 3,000 students, *"Make it your mission to make a difference."* Once you start to look for ways to make a difference, you will find little resistance or restrictions.

Leaders are the people who make a difference. They are big thinkers who understand that seeing things others do not see is not only a quality of leadership, but a responsibility, as well. Robert Frost said, *"Some men see things as they are and say, 'Why?' I dream of things that never were and say, 'Why not?'"*

Leaders use their vision to expand their mission and make a difference. Each of us has the ability to do likewise. For every action there is a reaction. Positive actions emit positive energy, which creates positive reactions. Conversely, the opposite is true. Take the story of a high school principal who awakens his wife one morning. Upset by long hours at her own work, she angrily tells him to make his own breakfast. The principal in turn yells at his secretary to get him coffee. Insulted, his secretary yells at the teachers while getting his coffee. *"Don't you have better things to do than sit in the lounge? You're the teachers; go teach!"*

The disgruntled teachers now go to their classrooms. One of the teachers tells a student named Pete, *"This is sloppy; not up to par."*

Well, Pete is now embarrassed as the class snickers. When he gets home, he goes right up to his younger brother, Repete, and throws him to the ground. *"What was that for?"* asks Repete.

"I just felt like it," says Pete.

Well, Repete is mad, so he kicks the dog, which then gets mad and chases the cat. The cat gets mad and chases the mouse. On, and on, and on.

B. J. Palmer said, *"Everything we think, say, or do will affect the lives of millions of people tomorrow."* What are you thinking? Saying? Doing? Napoleon said, *"Great men are meteors designed to burn so the earth may be lighted."*

My father was a leader, he would tell me *"Leaders LEAD."* He tried to teach me how to be a leader. My father was a great man, I have always tried to follow in his footsteps. As a young boy he would always hand me quotes on leadership. Today I'd like to spend "5 minutes" to share them with you. Here are some of my favorite leadership quotes:

The best executive is the one who has sense enough to pick good men to do what he wants done, and the self-restraint to keep from meddling with them while they do it.

Theodore Roosevelt

The task of leadership is not to put greatness into people, but to elicit it, for the greatness is there already.

John Buchan

The price of greatness is responsibility.

Winston Churchill

To lead people, walk beside them. As for the best leaders, the people do not notice their existence. The next best, the people honor and praise. The next, the people fear; and the next, the people hate. When the best leader's work is done the people say, "We did it ourselves!"

Lao-Tzu

Do not follow where the path may lead. Go instead where there is no path and leave a trail.

Harold R. McAlindon

If I have seen farther than others, it is because I was standing on the shoulder of giants.

Isaac Newton

I am a man of fixed and unbending principles, the first of which is to be flexible at all times.

Everett Dirksen

Leadership: the art of getting someone else to do something you want done because he wants to do it.

Dwight D. Eisenhower

Our chief want is someone who will inspire us to be what we know we could be.

Ralph Waldo Emerson

In times of change, learners inherit the Earth, while the learned find themselves beautifully equipped to deal with a world that no longer exists.

Eric Hoffer

I must follow the people. Am I not their leader?

Benjamin Disraeli

Example is not the main thing in influencing others, it is the only thing.

Albert Schweitzer

Leadership and learning are indispensable to each other.

John F. Kennedy

The final test of a leader is that he leaves behind him in other men, the conviction and the will to carry on.

Walter Lippman

If your actions inspire others to dream more, learn more, do more and become more, you are a leader.

John Quincy Adams

High sentiments always win in the end. The leaders who offer blood, toil, tears, and sweat always get more out of their followers than those who offer safety and a good time. When it comes to the pinch, human beings are heroic.

George Orwell

The key to successful leadership today is influence, not authority.

Kenneth Blanchard

The very essence of leadership is that you have to have vision. You can't blow an uncertain trumpet.

Theodore M. Hesburgh

I think leadership comes from integrity—that you do whatever you ask others to do. I think there are non-obvious ways to lead. Just by providing a good example as a parent, a friend, a neighbor makes it possible for other people to see better ways to do things. Leadership does not need to be a dramatic, fist in the air and trumpets blaring, activity.

Scott Berkun

Innovation distinguishes between a leader and a follower.

Steve Jobs

It is impossible to imagine anything which better becomes a ruler than mercy.

Seneca

The leaders who work most effectively, it seems to me, never say "I." And that's not because they have trained themselves not to say "I." They don't think "I." They think "we"; they think "team." They understand their job to be to make the team function. They accept responsibility and don't sidestep it, but "we" gets the credit. This is what creates trust, what enables you to get the task done.

Peter Drucker

Never doubt that a small group of thoughtful, concerned citizens can change world. Indeed, it is the only thing that ever has.

Margaret Mead

Let us not forget the criticism received by visionaries who predicted that the earth was round, or that man would walk on the moon, or that one day we would send pictures and letters instantly through telephone transmission. When President John F. Kennedy proposed putting a man on the moon, many laughed at him. Other countries had already ventured into space, but had no goal or even the vision to put a man on the moon. Kennedy had the vision and set the goal. He pushed the limits of exploration.

I cannot give you the formula for success, but I can give you the formula for failure, which is: Try to please everybody.

Herbert B. Swope

As a leader, it's your pressure to perform well and try to ensure having other's needs fulfilled at the same time. Sometimes it's a fine balance you walk, however. Herbert made a statement to a particular group of people: the people pleasers.

"People pleasers have the problem of insecurity. Because they are insecure in who they are as a leader, they take their judgment of who they are from their followers. They accept their followers' evaluation of who they are to be final.

You have to be ready to be unpopular. But as a leader, you must be ready to make unpopular decisions, and no doubt, turn a few people away from you sometimes.

You have to be secure enough to handle it and not be concerned about people's opinions.

If you're a leader or a public figure, criticism and sometimes harsh comments will not be a stranger to you. If you bend over for every person who has an opinion of you, you can be sure that you'll get nothing done at the end of the day".

It's okay if you don't please everyone as long as you please yourself. I am not saying you should be selfish, what I am saying is if you have a dream or an idea, don't let someone's negative thoughts steal your positive dreams.

King Camp Gillette was ridiculed and bankrupted when he set out to revolutionize one of the most common household tools. His invention was considered ridiculous. Not only was he unable to find investors, no mechanic would take on the job to create the prototype of his dream tool. Experienced mechanics, engineers, and even experts at the prestigious Massachusetts Institute of Technology all said that it couldn't be done. No one could make a razor sharp enough to give a good clean shave and make it cheap enough to justify throwing it away after it was worn down. It took Gillette four years to produce the first disposable blade and six more to get it on the market. In his first year of production, he only sold 51 blades at $5 each. Ten years work for $255. The second year he sold 90,844 blades and the concept of shaving was changed forever.

What if Gillette had given up? But, you see, he was sharp enough (pun intended) to realize that what he had was special and unique. Gillette was quoted as saying, *"If I had been a technically trained engineer, I would have quit."*

But Gillette was more than an engineer; he was a visionary and a leader. And he didn't stop reaching until he had achieved his goal and could be proud of his accomplishment and success. Lastly I leave you with this quote from Bill Gates. "As we look ahead into the next century, leaders will be those who empower others." Spend "5 minutes" today and everyday empowering yourself while leading others. The world is desperate for leadership. Maybe it is your turn to lead.

Winners are not those who never fail, but those who never quit.

Edwin Luis Cole

Chapter 10

"Don't Quit"

Winston Churchill became famous for his three word speech, ***"NEVER GIVE UP."*** I want to start our "5 minutes" today with a story and a poem.

> Sir Edmund Hillary was the first man to climb Mount Everest. On May 29, 1953 he scaled the highest mountain then known to man—29,000 feet straight up. He was knighted for his efforts. He even made American Express card commercials because of it! However, until we read his book, *High Adventure*, we don't understand that Hillary had to grow into this success.
>
> In 1952 Hillary attempted to climb Mount Everest, but failed. A few weeks later a group in England asked him to address its members. Hillary walked on stage to a thunderous applause. The audience was recognizing an attempt at greatness, but Edmund Hillary saw himself as a failure. He moved away from the microphone and walked to the edge of the platform. He made a fist, pointed at a picture of the mountain, and said in a loud voice, "Mount Everest, you beat me the first time, but I'll beat you the next time because you've grown all you are going to grow—but I'm still growing!"

Brian Cavanaugh, The Sower's Seeds

How many of you see yourselves as failures? You are not. You are an original. God has made no one like you. It's your uniqueness that separates you from the pack. The key is to find your dreams and "never give up." What do you want in life? What price are you willing to pay? Do you want to own your own business, to lose weight, to feel and look younger, to be smarter, more loved, more respected? The secrets to all these things are enclosed in this book, but you must keep reading, you can never stop moving forward, never stop believing in yourself, "never give up"

A frog was hopping around a farmyard, when it decided to investigate the barn. Being somewhat careless, and maybe a little too curious, he ended up falling into a pail half-filled with fresh milk.

As he swam about attempting to reach the top of the pail, he found that the sides of the pail were too high and steep to reach. He tried to stretch his back legs to push off the bottom of the pail but found it too deep. But this frog was determined not to give up, and he continued to struggle.

He kicked and squirmed and kicked and squirmed, until at last, all his churning about in the milk had turned the milk into a big hunk of butter. The butter was now solid enough for him to climb onto and get out of the pail!

The moral of the story? ***"Never Give Up!"***

Quitting may bring relief but it will never bring rewards.
                                                              Wes Beavis

Here is a poem by Wes Beavis, I hung in my sons' room when they were little. I read it often to them and with them. Print it, hang it on your wall, and email to all your friends.

Stay the Course

When things you confront do not go your way
That is basically how life is some days
You can sulk and think you want to quit
Or decide you will just get over it.
You are only as big as what gets you down,
Your size is measured by what makes you frown,
The mind of a fool is the mind that gives in
To thinking that quitting will help you to win.
You have been here before you know from your past,
No profit is gained by giving up on the task,
Whatever you do problems always exist
But you know they give way to those who persist.
Take one step forward from your problem and find
That you have moved on and left your problem behind,
Say to the challenge, 'I'm bigger than you,'
When you stay on your course you prove that it's true.

Author Unknown

Imagine, one man, one woman, one thought, one idea, can make a difference. Rosa Parks had a thought, which became a universal belief, and now a black man is president of the United States. It began with fight and commitment, one man willing to give up everything for the right and well-being of others, regardless of how harsh people acted toward him and treated him. I am talking about Abraham Lincoln. A man who was willing to risk the peace of our country for the basic principles of humanity. This man led no simple life and failed more often then he succeeded, but he was willing to put it all on the line, regardless of what other people thought, or said.

1816 He was forced from his home

1818 His mother died

1831 He failed in business

1832 He was defeated for State Legislature

1833 He failed in business again

1834 He was elected to State Legislature

1835 His fiancé died

1836 He suffered a nervous breakdown

1838 Defeated for State Legislature

1840 Defeated for Elector

1843 Defeated for Congress

1846 Elected to Congress

1848 He lost re-election

1854 He was rejected for land officer

1855 Defeated for Senate

1856 Defeated for Vice President

1858 Defeated for Senate

1860 Elected President of the United States

Lincoln was a man with a vision so strong that it took him 44 years of primarily failures, to not only succeed, but to lead our country to equality. In a lifetime of politics he had four times as many defeats as victories. Most men would have decided that life was unfair and given up. Lincoln never quit. Because Lincoln remained true to his goals, he eventually won the most important race of all.

Still think your failures are of great significance? Don't dwell on the times you failed to lose weight, quit smoking, or make a relationship work. Instead, spend the next "5 minutes" to concentrate on your goals. If you keep your eye on the green flag, instead of the sandtrap, you're halfway to winning the game.

Never Give Up!

What you get by achieving your goals is not as important as what you become by achieving your goals.

Zig Ziglar

Chapter 11

Goaltending

In "5 minutes" you can control your life by implementing your goals, affirming your affirmations, meditating instead of procrastinating, and by becoming proactive, not reactive.

In *Dying to Be Young*, we set daily goals during our recovery. We took action by combining our goals with our beliefs. Dennis Whatley said, "*The best kept secret of total success is that we must feel love inside of ourselves before we can give it to others.*"

Set "5 Minute" Goals to Succeed

Do you have difficulty setting goals for yourself and actually following through on them? Are you willing to invest "5 minutes" per day in setting goals? We all intend to reach our goals, but obstacles often get in our way. Here are a few quick tips for how to set goals to succeed.

1. Evaluate what is important in your life and what you would like to see improved.

2. Write your goals down. When you write them down, you can look at them every day and remind yourself of what you are trying to accomplish.

3. Make goals realistic.

4. Make goals timely. This will push you to do your best to reach them.

5. Stick with it! We oftentimes lose interest or motivation when working towards a goal. It's important to remember that long-term goals are not achieved overnight.

"5 Minute" Goals must be SMART

Specific. For example, "I want to lose weight." This is wishful thinking. It becomes a goal when I pin myself down to "I will lose 10 pounds in 30 days."

Measurable. If we cannot measure it, we cannot manage it. Measurement is a way of monitoring our progress.

Achievable. Achievable means that it should be out of reach enough to be challenging but it should not be out of sight, otherwise it becomes disheartening.

Realistic. Set goals you can achieve. A person who wants to lose 50 pounds in~30 days is being unrealistic.

Time-bound. There should be a starting date and a finishing date to every goal.

Suppose you have an entire football team, all eleven players, enthusiastically ready to play the game, all charged up, and then someone took the goal posts away. What would happen to the game? There is nothing left. How do you keep score? How do you know you have arrived? Goals give a sense of direction. Would you sit in a train or a plane without knowing where it was going? The obvious answer is no.

Then why do people go through life without having any goals?

I tell my children that the vitamin of friendship is B1. If you want a friend, you must be one, setting a goal to be a good friend is a real, attainable goal. If you need a friend, you must be one. In order to be the person that you are, you must reflect on the person that you have been. Who in your life—mother, father, brother, sister, teacher, preacher—told you that you were not capable of greatness? Who told you that you were a mediocre student or that you were not capable of success? We reviewed and will continue to review the likes of Thomas Edison, Henry Ford, and Winston Churchill—people who made a great impact on our lives and lives around the world. Yet none of these people were recognized as being destined to succeed. They were not cultivated, they were not born into success. They achieved it the old-fashioned way and they worked for it. Often during their lives they were looked upon as weeds that the system tried to snuff out as it tried to grow a more "successful" type of crop. But these people all had a commonality: each had a propensity for success. A propensity for success that was so great that they were able to listen to their inner voice, known as the super-conscious, which told them what they could do. People are not always right, and you are not always wrong. You must see that many times through failure comes success. And many times, success can lead to failure. But you must recognize your own ability to change, that you can alter your destiny by altering your mindset, by setting smart goals. William James said, "*We cannot always control our circumstances, but we can control our thoughts during these circumstances. By controlling our thoughts, we can create more productive future circumstances.*"

I can't overemphasize the importance of goal setting. The key to goal getting is goal setting. If you don't set it, you're less apt to get it.

Let me share with you a story by author Napoleon Hill, from his bestselling book, *Think And Grow Rich*. The author shares case histories of many great people. Few of these people were born beautiful, rich, or incredibly talented. The one thing these individuals had in common, however, was a burning desire to succeed. Take the story of Edward C.

Barnes, who was determined to become a business associate of the great Thomas Edison, thus he set a personal goal to attain this desire.

Barnes was not a scientist, nor was he a wealthy man. And there were two obstacles to his goal: One, he had never met Edison. Two he lacked the train fare to New Jersey where Edison lived.

Barnes could have given up, in which case you wouldn't be reading about him right now. Instead, he made his way to a startled but impressed Edison.

"He stood there before me looking like an ordinary tramp, but there was something in the expression of his face which conveyed the impression that he was determined to get what he had come after. I had learned from my years of experiences with men that when a man really desires a thing so deeply that he is willing to stake his entire future on the single turn of the wheel in order to get it, he is sure to win. I gave him the opportunity he asked for because I saw he made up his mind to stand by until he succeeded."

Subsequent events proved Edison correct. Edison had perfected a new office device which was to become known as the Edison Dictating Machine. At the time he met Barnes, he was having difficulty getting people to market the invention. His sales force simply wasn't enthusiastic. Barnes took over the job and sold the machine so successfully that Edison gave him an exclusive contract to sell, market, and distribute the Edison Dictating Machine. The rest is history.

Taking "5 minutes" per day, to work on your goals is important, but spending 24 hours per day committed to your goals is the key. Barnes set a goal for himself and even Edison knew and realized nothing would stop him. This demonstrates the power of commitment. You must believe in yourself. Say daily affirmations, set goals, and implement them into your life.

Don't discuss your problems unless you want to reinforce your weaknesses. Don't make excuses unless you are willing to excuse yourself from that circle of friends. Successful people seek to surround themselves with those who smell of success. Be positive and positive things will enter into your consciousness.

Remember, the mind cannot tell the difference between real experiences and those that are vividly and repeatedly imagined. Be a dreamer and follow your dreams. Set goals. A goal without a plan is nothing more than a wish. Set a goal and set forth a plan, then establish affirmations. Affirm your goals. Affirm your uniqueness. Affirm your creativity. Affirm your spontaneity. Affirm your cleverness. Affirm your personality. Affirm your health. Affirm your desire. Affirm your propensity to succeed. Affirm your desire to win. Affirm your desire to be a good person. Affirm your strength. Affirm your love for your family. Affirm your love for yourself. To receive affirmations and other bonuses, go to www.5minutemotivator.com.

Napoleon once said that imagination rules the world. Einstein believed that imagination is more important than knowledge, for knowledge is limited to all we know and understand at the present, while imagination embraces the entire world and all there ever will be to know and understand. It is our dreams that create our goals. Remember, *"goal setters are goal getters."*

We must look to ourselves, to our inner eye that sees us in a way that no one else sees us, and affirm our uniqueness. Once we know who we are, it's easier to decide where we want to go. When we get in the car and plan to go to the store, isn't that a form of goal setting? We set a goal and then we affirm our commitment to get there. Once you set this goal only you, can stop you, from reaching your desired destination.

Since the beginning of the world, it's estimated that 11 billion people have walked the face of the earth, and no two have ever been the same. It's your uniqueness that has carried you this far. Spend just "5 minutes" a day to review your goals, affirmations, and to be a dreamer. As Jiminy Cricket in Pinocchio said, *"Accentuate the positive, eliminate the negative."*

Consider these goal setters who stuck to their goals regardless of any adversity:

- After **Fred Astaire's** first screen test, the memo from the testing director of MGM said, *"Can't act. Can't sing. Balding. Can dance a little."* Astaire kept that memo over the fireplace of his Beverly Hills home.

- An expert said of **Vince Lombardi,** *"He possesses minimal football knowledge, lacks motivation."*

- **Socrates** was called *an immoral corrupter of youth.*

- **Louisa May Alcott,** author of *Little Women,* was encouraged to find work as a servant or seamstress by her family.

- **Beethoven** handled a violin awkwardly and preferred creating his own compositions to improving his technique. His teacher called him a *"hopeless composer."* He continued to compose even though he went deaf.

- The parents of the famous opera singer **Enrico Caruso** wanted him to become an engineer. His teacher said he had no voice at all.

- **Charles Darwin,** the father of the theory of evolution, gave up a medical career and was told by his father, *"You care for nothing but shooting dogs and rat-catching."* In his autobiography, Darwin wrote, *"I was considered by all my masters, and by my father, a very ordinary boy, rather below the common standard of intellect."*

- **Walt Disney** was fired by a newspaper editor for lack of ideas. He also went bankrupt several times.

- **Albert Einstein** did not speak until he was four years old and did not read until he was seven. His teacher described him as mentally slow, unsociable, and adrift forever in his false dreams. He was expelled from one school and refused admittance to the Zurich Polytechnic School.

• **Louis Pasteur** was recognized as only a mediocre pupil in undergraduate studies and ranked 15th out of 22 in chemistry class.

• **Isaac Newton** did very poorly in grade school.

• The sculptor **Rodin's** father said, *"I have an idiot for a son."* Described as the worst pupil in school, Rodin failed three times to secure admittance to the school of art. His uncle called him uneducable.

• **Leo Tolstoy**, author of *War and Peace*, flunked out of college. He was described as unable and unwilling to learn.

• Playwright **Tennessee Williams** was enraged when his play, *Me, Vasha*, was not chosen in a class competition at Washington University where he was a student in English. The teacher recalls that Williams denounced the judges' choices and their intelligence.

• **F. W. Woolworth's** employees at the dry goods store claimed that he did not have enough sense to wait upon customers.

• **Henry Ford** failed and went broke five times before he finally succeeded.

• **Babe Ruth**, considered by many sports historians to be the greatest athlete of all time, is famous for setting the home run record of 714 home runs. He also holds the record for strike-outs: Babe Ruth struck out over 3,000 times.

- **Winston Churchill** failed 6th grade. He did not become Prime Minister of England until he was 62 and only then after a lifetime of defeats and setbacks. His greatest contributions came when he was a senior citizen.

- Eighteen publishers turned down **Richard Bach's** 10,000-word story about a soaring seagull, *Jonathan Livingston Seagull*, before Macmillan finally published it in 1970. By 1975, it had sold more than 7,000,000 copies in the United States alone.

- **Richard Herker** worked 7 years on his humorous war novel, *M.A.S.H.*, only to have it rejected by 21 publishers before Morrow decided to publish it. It became a runaway bestseller, spawning a blockbuster movie and a highly successful television series.

What have we learned from this chapter? We need to spend "5 minutes" per day setting goals, working on our goals, and saying our affirmations, and 24 hours per day staying committed to our goals and not to letting anyone or anything stand in the way of our success or our destiny.

Winning isn't everything, but the will to win is everything.
Vince Lombardi

Chapter 12

The Winner Within

We have often heard of the Pareto Principle, not because of its name, but in association with the numbers it represents. The Pareto principle is also known as the 80/20 rule. This represents:

That 20% of the people take up 80% of our time.
That 20% of the time brings in 80% of results.
That 20% of the book contains 80% of the content.
That 20% of our work gives us 80% of our satisfaction.
That 20% of the presentation produces 80% of the impact.
That 20% of the people will give 80% of the money.
That 20% of the people will make 80% of the decisions.
That 20% of the people will eat 80% of the food.
That 20% of the people will pay 80% of the world's taxes.
That 20% of the class will ask 80% of the questions.
At work, 20% of the staff will produce 80% of the problems.

When you realize that 20% of your priorities will you give you 80% of your production, then you must spend your time, energy, money, and personal issues on the top 20% of your priorities because your priorities will be equivalent to your production. You must either organize or agonize. Most people do not have the ability to handle more than one project at a time, so put your projects in order and prioritize your work, your family, and your time. Prioritize based on importance and urgency.

High priority/high urgency is when the boss gives you an assignment and says, *"I need it today."* High priority/low urgency is when the boss gives you an assignment, but does not set a deadline. Time management is an important aspect of the Pareto formula and we must recognize that we need to utilize our time wisely. Every person is either reactive or proactive. Every person is either a thermometer or a thermostat. Leaders initiate— followers react. Leaders lead by example—followers wait and respond. Leaders pick up the phone—followers wait for the phone to ring. Leaders spend time resolving and anticipating problems—followers spend time reacting to the problem. Leaders spend time with people—followers follow people, not making use of the time. Pablo Picasso said, "Every child is an artist. The problem is how to remain an artist once that child grows up." Why is it that we are born positive, not fearing failure? We are not afraid to take our first steps. Recognizing that we will probably fall, we stumble, fall down, and get back up again. I have noticed that the Pareto formula is not something defined at birth because 20% of the children aren't going to walk 80% of the time; they will eventually walk 100% of the time. Remember, every action you take is either weak or strong, and when every action is strong, we are successful and we win.

Winners vs. Losers

Winners always have an idea, **Losers** *always have an excuse.*
Winners always say, "I'll do it," **Losers** *always say, "It's not my job."*
Winners always see an answer for every problem, **Losers** *always see a problem for every answer.*
Winners always say, "I can," **Losers** *always say, "I can't."*
Winners always look for a way to do it, **Losers** *always look for a way to get out of it.*

Henry Ford said, "*Whether you think you can or think you can't, you're right.*"

I believe that 20% of the content of this book will provide you with 80% of the information that you need to be successful. You do not have to agree with everything I say. An axiom that I have lived by and learned is, "*Even a clock that doesn't work is right twice a day.*"

We need to realize that we need to be positive people; I say, be a "thumbs up" person.

"5 Minute" Commandments for Success

1. Picture the positives.

2. Eliminate the negatives.

3. Focus on your strengths.

4. Eliminate your limits.

5. Meditate.

6. Plan with positive people.

7. Ride elevators with the elevated.

8. Remember there is only one you in the universe!

9. Live your dreams, not someone else's.

10. Throw "*never,*" "*won't,*" and "*can't*" out of your vocabulary.

Teach your Inner Winner to believe in yourself, in your ability to win regardless of the situation. Spend "5 minutes" now affirming your Inner Winner.

I believe I have the power and potential that the world has never even come close to realizing.

I believe I have far more intelligence than I have ever used.

I believe I am more creative than I have ever imagined.

I believe the greatest achievements of my life lie ahead of me.

I believe the happiest moments of my life are yet to come.

I believe my greatest successes are still waiting for me on the road ahead.

I believe I can solve any problem, overcome any obstacle and achieve any goal I set my mind to.

I believe that if it is to be, it's up to me.

I believe the key to success is faith in oneself. From this day forward let's spend "5 minutes" per day building our faith muscles. Tony Robbins once asked an audience, *"What are your fundamental beliefs?"* What are your core feelings that you truly believe about yourself? What are your faiths? If you fundamentally believe the world conspires with you, that is a completely different belief than the world conspires against you. Imagine your will, your strength, your optimism, if you fundamentally believe in yourself. Imagine knowing and believing in a faith sort of way that you will always succeed, no matter what the situation.

The beauty in all this insight is that you can change one minute, one day at a time. Tony Robbins gives a very simple way to build and grow your faith muscles:

Step 1. See things the way they are—don't ignore reality.

Step 2. See things as they could be—see them a better way.

Step 3. Take action to make it happen.

This "5 minute" exercise will allow us to see ***The Way Things Are, The Way Things Should Be, and the Way You Want Things to Be.*** By changing yourself, "5 minutes" at a time, you'll build your faith muscles and then you'll make things happen. Yes, you can change your life simply by changing yourself, "5 minutes" at a time.

If you put yourself in a position where you have to stretch outside your comfort zone, then you are forced to expand your consciousness.

Les Brown

Chapter 13

The Zone

The Zone is more than a best-selling diet book; it's a spiritual place we all seek. This place resides within us, waiting to manifest itself at our command. My mother once shared with me a special poem when I was a little boy, "Live your life as if it were a field covered with snow, for wherever you walk, your steps will show."

It only takes "5 minutes" a day to decide whether you are a winner or a loser, whether you are a hero or a zero, whether you are the victor or the victim. But in those "5 minutes" a day, you can sit down and formulate your plan. Are you one of the 20% that are proactive or one of the 80% that are reactive? If you find yourself in the 80% group, ask yourself this question, "Are you chained there? Or, do you have the ability to change your position by changing your attitude? It starts within. If you make friends with yourself, you will never be alone because happiness comes from within, not from the outside. When you recognize that you cannot continue to function in a manner that you do not believe is true to yourself, then you have discovered your own self-worth and your own potential. A leader's attitude is caught by his or her followers more quickly than are his or her actions. It's impossible to have bad thoughts or a bad attitude and still maintain success. Norman Vincent Peale, who put a prayer in my first book, *Lifestyle of the Fit and Famous*, relates a story in his book, *Power of the Plus Factor*.

Once walking through the twisted little streets of Kowloon in Hong Kong, I came upon a tattoo studio. In the window were displayed samples of the tattoos available. On the chest or arm, you could tattoo an anchor, flag, or mermaid, but what struck me with force was the three words that could be tattooed on one's flesh, 'Born to Lose.'

I entered the shop in astonishment. I pointed to those words and asked the Chinese tattoo artist, "Does anybody really have that terrible phrase, *Born to Lose*, tattooed on their body?"

He replied, "Yes, sometimes."

"But," I said, "I just can't believe that anyone in his right mind would do that."

The Chinese man simply tapped his forehead and in broken English said, "Before tattoo on body, tattoo on mind."

In a world influenced by the likes of Dennis Rodman, who expresses himself on his body, I wonder—if we tattoo our mind, saying that we are born to lose instead of born to win, what are our chances for success? The chances for long-term accomplishment are diminished because people sabotage themselves. In golf, it's called the "yips." Why is it that so many professional performers can perform on the practice putting green to excellence, and then at the time of the event, they self-defeat their practice? Maybe it's because they feel that they don't deserve to win? It's my belief that we were all put on this earth to win.

One of my favorite golfers is Arnold Palmer. I live in a golf course community called PGA National, and I have had the opportunity to attend the PGA Championships. I was chosen as chiropractor one year for this prestigious tournament and had the opportunity to work and walk with many of the golfers. There was nothing more flavorful and fascinating than "Arnie's Army." "Arnie's Army" can still be counted among the young and old. This great golfer, throughout the course of this week, never flaunted his success. He signed autographs, hats, and golf balls. Here is a man who, although he has won hundreds of trophies and awards, has been recognized by presidents and dignitaries throughout the world, never ceasing to put on a happy face. Even after overcoming prostate surgery, Arnold Palmer was there, smiling and shaking hands, and still giving autographs. I was told that with all the trophies that Arnold Palmer has won, he only keeps one in his office: a battered little cup that he got for his first professional win at the Canadian Open in 1955. In addition to that cup, he has a framed plaque on the wall and the plaque tells one why he has been successful. It reads:

> If you think you are beaten, you are. If think you dare not, you don't. If you like to win, but think you can't, it is almost certain you won't. Life's battles don't always go to the stronger or faster man, but sooner or later the man who wins is the man who thinks he can.

This year, thanks to my good friend and partner Dr. Gerry Mattia, I got to meet Arnold Palmer and get the picture I so desired. He was everything I wrote about him and more, the consummate ambassador of the game of golf and a gentleman in the game of life.

Winning in life, is getting the "hole in one" that is created by hard work, endless effort, sacrifice and discipline.

The Zone is the difference between the golfer who wins or loses. It's that special place where we feel invincible and in total control. To many in the golf world, there was a time when Tiger Woods was invincible. He won week after week, often with a miraculous ending. He appeared almost inhuman. Almost everyone believed he would break the records for total winnings and winnings of major tournaments held by Jack Nicklaus. Now, many believe he will never achieve this goal which was once so close. With all of Tiger Woods' talent, he does not win every week; lately, he has not won at all. Now, beset by injuries and personal problems, he appears almost mortal. He has lost that special place where he lived for many years—invincible. We call it "being in the zone," the feeling that we have the ability to move forward and win. We have the ability to make a difference. We have the ability to succeed, and this success starts within. As Tiger works to get his life back, he continues to seek that place of comfort we call The Zone. To be there, to get there, you have to be happy with yourself. If you are not, change what you don't like and you are on the road to The Zone. If you want to find your way into The Zone, here are 24 things to remember.

24 Things To Remember

Collin McCarty

"Your presence is a present to the world.
You're unique and one of a kind.
Your life can be what you want it to be.
Take the days just one at a time.
Count your blessings, not your troubles.
You'll make it through whatever comes along.
Within you are so many answers.
Understand, have courage, be strong.
Don't put limits on yourself.
So many dreams are waiting to be realized.
Decisions are too important to leave to chance.
Reach for your peak, your goal, your prize.
Nothing wastes more energy than worrying.
The longer one carries a problem, the heavier it gets.
Don't take things too seriously.
Live a life of serenity, not a life of regrets.
Remember that a little love goes a long way…
Remember that a lot…goes forever.
Remember that friendship is a wise investment.
Life's treasures are people…together.
Realize that it's never too late.

Do ordinary things in an extraordinary way.
Have health and hope and happiness.
Take time to wish upon a star.
And don't ever forget…for even a day…
How very special you are.

It only takes "5 minutes" a day to plant the seeds of success, the seeds of greatness. And if we are to succeed by planting these seeds, then we must weed out the negatives in our life. If we allow these weeds to grow, they will strangle all that is good within us and then we will be without. We must plan our "5 minutes" daily, setting our goals, stating our affirmations, and moving into our zone.

My recommendations are that you choose a time and space where you will not be interrupted and where you can let yourself relax. Physical and mental relaxation is mandatory. I find that the best position is lying down or reclining with the feet elevated and uncrossed. The back should be straight and the hands either at our sides or on our left. Soft music or other tranquil sounds such as nature sounds or any music without words may also be helpful. (I like Bach, Beethoven, Bell, Vivaldi, and Mozart.) Relaxation is key, coupled with breathing and concentration on our bodies. We must start with every muscle and fiber in our body by taking a breath in through the nose for a count of 3 seconds, holding it in for 3 seconds, and letting it out over 5 seconds. We must start talking—self-talk, inner talk—to build our self-esteem.

Affirm to yourself as you meditate into a spiritual zone, "*My breathing is relaxed and effortless. My heartbeat is slow and regular. My muscles are healthy, strong, and relaxed. I am relaxed. I am at peace. I am in control of my body. God put me on this planet to succeed. I am unique. I am special. I would rather be me than anyone else in the world. I feel my body is healthier today than it was yesterday. The best time in life is now. I am proud of my accomplishments and my goals. I will learn from my successes and my failures. I will earn the respect of others by leading by example. I am at peace.*

I relish every second of every minute of every day.

"*I look at children and realize there is still a child in me. I am a winner. I was born to succeed; I was born to lead. I will create success within myself and within others. I respect and appreciate myself. There is no better day than today. I thank God for life; I am at peace in mind, body, spirit, soul. I am relaxed. I am a child of God.*"

By utilizing this relaxation, affirmation, and goal-setting technique once a day, it will turn your coffee break into a health break. The affirmation that I just described can be adapted into your own words, but it's something that must be done every day. Your "5 minutes" today spent using the right tools will unlock the combination of success that exists in each and every one of our spirits, moving everyone toward that special place of peace and wellness—The Zone.

It isn't until you come to a spiritual understanding of who you are - not necessarily a religious feeling, but deep down, the spirit within—that you can begin to take control.

Oprah Winfrey

Chapter 14

Take Control of Your Life

In today's world of schedules, phones, cell phones, e-mails, and texting, people often feel that their unhappiness is based upon losing control. Losing control of their time does not mean losing control of their destiny. We must decide that the things that matter most in life do not have to be held hostage to those that matter the least. According to a recent issue of *Time* magazine, we are living in a period called "time famine." Life is becoming more complex. Many people feel that their life is a treadmill. But we have a choice. Our life does not have to be a saga, nor does our life have to be a treadmill. Our life should be a quest, a journey. But we have to take control of the reins of life in order to control its direction. A recent research study reported, the average American spends 4.5 hours a day watching television. In essence, that means that the average child spends more time with their television set than they do with their parents. The demands of today's marketplace put extraordinary demands upon almost any employee or employer. If you are not productive, you are out. This puts tremendous pressure on the average American to perform, and thus creates tremendous levels of anxiety. Last year, five billion dollars was spent on anti-depressant drugs. That alone is depressing. Why would we, in a world of such abundance, be so depressed? Possibly, it's the increasing time demands of our careers that affect our personal lives.

Our lives are so filled with things we must do, with things we should do, not to mention things we want to do, that often we feel trapped. Literally, we sometimes feel paralyzed, unable to do anything. Many people feel that they are working harder and longer, yet accomplishing less. More and more employees are eating lunch at their desk rather than spending an hour out, often working harder and achieving less.

Everybody wants to be in control; this is one of the innate desires of all human beings. There is no worse feeling than being out of control, sensing that other people or external circumstances are governing what we do. Often, we feel like puppets on a string, controlled by other people's time, other people's schedules, other people's thoughts, or other people's emotions, not realizing that we ourselves have total control. When something or someone else controls our lives, this tends to yank us from side to side like a puppet on a string. When we are manipulated, we cannot be happy. We must take back control of our lives to control our destiny. We will never experience inner peace if we cannot experience inner control. This chapter focuses on gaining back control, converting time into energy, energy into happiness, and happiness into peace.

In order to understand the laws of time, we must also parallel our minds to the laws of nature. These laws do not vary, and they influence us on a day-to-day basis. One such law is the law of aerodynamics. Now that we know that the Wright brothers were not wrong, we must look at how man has not reinvented the law of aerodynamics, but has modified this technology to the point that air travel is the primary means of business and personal travel. Now we can safely fly people all over the world, at any given minute and on any given day. Our planes can hold hundreds of people and safely transport them all because we understand the law of aerodynamics.

Then there is the law of sound. We can take a musician's best work and, through the use of a computer, transform it into digital codes, print those codes onto palm-sized discs, and then read and translate those codes back into their original sound by laser and computer technology. Instead of hearing isolated or random electronic noises, we can sit in our living room and enjoy the beauty of Beethoven, Bach, Mozart, or for my son's pleasure, John Mayer. We are able to reproduce and transport these sounds to living rooms around the world because we understand some of the laws of nature.

One law that still baffles me is the law of energy. The illusion is that our lives are controlled by time, while in reality they are controlled by energy. Energy is the commodity that elicits the difference of life versus death. In Florida, after the terrible Hurricane Andrew that hit the Miami/Kendall area, Andrew's destruction of electric and power systems robbed us of basic necessities such as running water, electrical power, and in some cases, even a roof over our heads, which literally transformed the inhabitants instantly from modern times to frontier times. We must appreciate what we have without first having to lose it. Energy is something we cannot see, and therefore take for granted. We can feel it; we know it exists. Man can harness the mighty ocean's waves and transform them into electricity. He can harness water and transform it into electricity. Windmills are still used as a way to harness energy in some areas of the world. So, by understanding natural laws, the laws of the universe, we can encapsulate these laws and empower ourselves into our everyday life. You see, our collective understanding of these laws is impressive. We know how to turn on the fan. We know how to bring Beethoven into the living room. We even know now how to get onto the Internet to book a plane trip. Yet our personal understanding of these laws is neophytic.

Learn how to adapt to your environment and utilize the laws of nature, and recognize that we don't have to invent the automobile, that we don't have to invent electricity, and that these conveniences are at our fingertips to elevate and improve our very existence. They are not meant to isolate us in front of a screen, watching soap operas, wondering if it's day or night. This is not the essence of our existence. The essence of our existence is to learn, to create. But our entire existence must be in accordance with the laws of nature and happiness. One of the great motivational speakers Zig Ziglar, offers his *30 Qualities for Success. Spend "5 minutes" now to score yourself from 1 to 30 and see how many you possess:*

Honesty, Humor, Friendliness, Confidence,
Integrity, Persistence, Humility, Goal Setter,
Decisive, Hard Worker, Learner,
Positive Mental Attitude, Compassionate,
Disciplined, Dedicated, Faithful,
Dependable, Knowledgeable, Communicator,
Loving, Enthusiastic, Motivated, Patient,
Loyal, Organized, Good Listener,
Empathetic, Self-Respect,
Common Sense, and Character.

What was your score? We should spend "5 minutes" per day to work on our success qualities. We must all work to possess these qualities. If you're not happy, spend "5 minutes" a day studying the secrets to happiness. Anyone can learn how to be happy, even without being anywhere near the achievement of your goals. Winning and achieving your goals takes time, the fact that you are working on your goals puts you in control of your future.

It's important to stay and become positive and happy if you want to change any aspect of your life.

Without changing your state of mind, you will not be able to move from where you are now to where you want to be.

It's impossible to find happiness outside of yourself and it's better to not even attempt to do that—happiness is an inside job.

If you try to find happiness in something other than yourself, you'll be disappointed because you will realize that nothing or no one else can give happiness to you.

Yes, there are times you may temporarily become happy by using an external excuse such as shopping or finding a new partner. But such happiness is always temporary. You can't buy happiness; you must cultivate it to control it.

The only way to find true happiness that lasts forever is by searching for it inside yourself, by being honest with yourself. What you focus on daily brings out those features in yourself and others. The key is to pay attention only to things that make you happy or that are pleasant to your senses; you'll eventually bring out those features in yourself.

This way you will start attracting other positive things and events into your life because they will resonate with who you have become. The proof of your absolute control of your happiness will make you confident and relaxed. That's how the true happiness will come into your reality and stay there. It's good to aspire to greatness. Although not a religious man, I read this once in a locker room that a coach had put on the bulletin board for his team. The words below are more than religious in nature—they are spiritual and speak to the core of achieving personal excellence.

In the world of spiritual endeavor;
as in the world of athletic competition,
we must learn never to be content
with the level we have reached
but, with the help of God
and with our own determined efforts,
we must aim at ever greater heights,
at continual improvement,
so that we
may in the end reach maturity,
'the measure of the stature
of the fullness of Christ.'

Pope John XXIII

Take "5 minutes" now to take control of your life. Here are 5 ways that you can do it "5 minutes" per day.

1. **Reorganizing your thoughts.** It can be hard to see things the way they really are if your mind is focused on the "what ifs" and "should haves." Letting go of the negative energy in your life is a great start. Organize your thoughts by organizing your goals. Only you can take control of who you are, what you do, and what you think. So, keep your attitude high and eliminate the negative. STOP focusing on something you can't control, it simply relinquishes your hold on life. Worrying doesn't change a thing, so why not take control of your thoughts?

2. **Staying on schedule.** Getting back into your daily routine can help you regain some of the control you think you may have lost. Try to always be "5 minutes" early. The reality is you are always in control. If you've been feeling like everything has been changing, keep yourself in check by going about life as normal. Remember if you're always "5 minutes" early, you're never late. This "5 minute" habit might just give you the confidence you need to move forward! Remember

3. **Giving yourself a positive mantra.** Maybe you have a favorite chapter in this book, or a comforting song that you find uplifting. Maybe there's a quote you read that moved you. Write it down and put it in your wallet, on your mirror, on your desk, or anywhere close to you to remind you of the feeling you had when you first read it. All you need sometimes is a positive reinforcement of the good things in your life to keep you going. A cliché line that I've used many times is "Life goes on in spite of yourself." Remembering that line or anything else that seems to ring true with you is important to make sure you're always keeping the faith.

4. **Surrounding yourself with positive influences.** Eliminate negative influences in your life. Life is too short to let others

bring you down or keep the negative in your life. Once you learn to like yourself, once you develop faith, faith in yourself, you'll realize you're never alone. Embrace those around you that have a positive influence on you. Remember friends love you for who you are, not what you have.

5. **Be yourself.** Never forget who you are and where you came from. I'm from Jersey City, New Jersey and proud of it. Be proud of your past, for it made you the person you are today. The key to success is to know that you're in control every moment of every day. Be proud of who you are for you're unique. God made you in his image and there are no duplicates. You are who you are, so be proud of who you are and where you came from. If that seems difficult, revert back to the past four steps. It's important to see yourself for who you are and that you are in total control of your life, rather than to think that the one in control isn't you. You're always in control of your own destiny. E.E. Cummings said, "*To be nobody but yourself in a world which is doing its best, night and day, to make you everybody else, means to fight the hardest battle which any human being can fight, and never stop fighting.*"

The Constitution only gives people the right to pursue happiness. You have to catch it yourself.

Benjamin Franklin

Chapter 15

Please Yourself First

To learn how to be happy, you should try to please yourself as often as you can. You should do things you enjoy doing, things that relax you and put you in a better mood. If you like to read, write, knit, play golf, play with your children—then do it. Perhaps your happiness may be found in things such as meditation, eating food you love, being with good friends, taking a nice bath, exercising, sleeping, dressing well, etc.

The more joyful things you do, the more positive you become, and the more good things you will attract into your life.

You can't change your current circumstances if you don't change your mindset. Focus only on the best things in life and your reality will change because you've raised your attitude. Because you've been in the same state of mind for a very long time, your reality won't change instantly. Spend "5 minutes" every day focusing on your happiness. You have to change your old reality, and then grow out of your old reality and into the new one you're creating.

You should focus daily on even the smallest signs showing that your reality, your mindset, is changing. The happier you are about them, the better chance that bigger and better changes will come into your life.

It's the little things in life that make the largest difference. Small signs can be as simple as receiving an unexpected call from an old friend, an invitation to some party, or just the feeling of being happy for no reason. This is an indication that you're about to change your reality into a more positive one. Many people find it strange when they start feeling good without any reason, and their ego, which is their limited beliefs, moves them out of this happiness and makes them miserable again. A wonderful book to read is *The Four Agreements* by Don Miguel Ruiz. When I took over Nutrisystem on Wall Street and was made President and COO of a publically traded company, I handed a copy to all my board members. A happy person is a successful person; a happy company is a successful company.

Reading positive books will take you to positive places in your mind. Have you ever had a day where you just wake up happy?

Now your ego kicks in because you start paying attention to this present moment, rather than focusing on your mind. You start hearing a voice in your head that says, *What are you so happy about? There's nothing you should be joyful for. You didn't achieve anything you planned for today. You don't like where you live and your life is nowhere near where you want it to be.*

After hearing that voice you start feeling doubtful about your feeling of happiness and it vanishes from your mind. You start feeling as you always did, a bit fearful and unhappy with where you are. When this or similar situation plays out and you give in to your old habits, you stop happiness and a better future from reaching you. Back to square one. Unless you kick negativity in the eye with positive affirmations. Yes, you can change your thoughts, your consciousness, and your mind.

Let me share some things I've learned from an unknown author.

I've learned—that you cannot make someone love you. All you can do is be someone who can be loved. The rest is up to them.

I've learned—that no matter how much I care, some people just don't care back.

I've learned—that it takes years to build up trust, and only seconds to destroy it.

I've learned—that it's not what you have in your life, but who you have in your life that counts.

I've learned—that you can get by on charm for about 15 minutes. After that, you'd better know something.

I've learned—that you shouldn't compare yourself to the best others can do.

I've learned—that it's not what happens to people that's important. It's what they do about it, but do the best you can do.

I've learned—that you can do something in an instant that will give you heartache for life.

I've learned—that no matter how thin you slice it, there are always two sides.

I've learned—that it's taking me a long time to become the person I want to be.

I've learned—that it's a lot easier to react than it is to think.

I've learned—that you should always leave loved ones with loving words. It may be the last time you see them.

I've learned—that you can keep going long after you think you can't.

I've learned—that we are responsible for what we do, no matter how we feel.

I've learned—that either you control your attitude or it controls you.

I've learned—that regardless of how hot and steamy a relationship is at first, the passion fades and there had better be something else to take its place.

I've learned—that heroes are the people who do what has to be done when it needs to be done, regardless of the consequences.

I've learned—that learning to forgive takes practice.

I've learned—that there are people who love you dearly, but just don't know how to show it.

I've learned—that money is a lousy way of keeping score.

I've learned—that my best friend and I can do anything, or nothing, and have the best time.

I've learned—that sometimes the people you expect to kick you when you're down will be the ones to help you get back up.

I've learned—that sometimes when I'm angry I have the right to be angry, but that doesn't give me the right to be cruel.

I've learned—that true friendship continues to grow, even over the longest distance. Same goes for true love.

I've learned—that just because someone doesn't love you the way you want them to doesn't mean they don't love you with all they have.

I've learned—that maturity has more to do with what types of experiences you've had and what you've learned from them, and less to do with how many birthdays you've celebrated.

I've learned—that you should never tell a child their dreams are unlikely or outlandish. Few things are more humiliating, and what a tragedy it would be if they believed it.

I've learned—that your family won't always be there for you. It may seem funny, but people you aren't related to can take care of you and love you and teach you to trust people again. Families aren't biological.

I've learned—that no matter how good a friend is, they're going to hurt you every once in a while and you must forgive them for that.

I've learned—that it isn't always enough to be forgiven by others. Sometimes you have to learn to forgive yourself.

I've learned—that no matter how bad your heart is broken the world doesn't stop for your grief.

I've learned—that our background and circumstances may have influenced who we are, but we are responsible for who we become.

I've learned—that sometimes when my friends fight, I'm forced to choose sides even when I don't want to.

I've learned—that just because two people argue, it doesn't mean they don't love each other. And just because they don't argue, it doesn't mean they do.

I've learned—that sometimes you have to put the individual ahead of their actions.

I've learned—that we don't have to change friends if we understand that friends change.

I've learned—that you shouldn't be so eager to find out a secret. It could change your life forever.

I've learned—that two people can look at the exact same thing and see something totally different.

I've learned—that no matter how you try to protect your children, they will eventually get hurt and you will hurt in the process.

I've learned—that there are many ways of falling and staying in love.

I've learned—that no matter the consequences, those who are honest with themselves get farther in life.

I've learned—that no matter how many friends you have, if you are their pillar you will feel lonely and lost at the times you need them most.

I've learned—that your life can be changed in a matter of hours by people who don't even know you.

I've learned—that even when you think you have no more to give, when a friend cries out to you, you will find the strength to help.

I've learned—that writing, as well as talking, can ease emotional pains.

I've learned—that the paradigm we live in is not all that is offered to us.

I've learned—that credentials on the wall do not make you a decent human being.

I've learned—that the people you care most about in life are taken from you too soon.

I've learned—that although the word "love" can have many different meanings, it loses value when overly used.

I've learned—that it's hard to determine where to draw the line between being nice and not hurting people's feelings and standing up for what you believe.

Take "5 minutes" right now to write down what you've learned and what you're willing to incorporate in your life. No matter where you are in life, the key is to be happy.

"5 Minutes" to Be Happy With Where You Are

The grass is not always greener on the other side. So often we wish we were there instead of here. But once we get there, there is now here. Take "5 minutes" a day to just enjoy the moment, to enjoy yourselves. Norman Vincent Peale said, "It is of practical value to learn to like yourself. Since you must spend so much time with yourself you might as well get some satisfaction out of the relationship."

Even if your present circumstances are really bad and you're nowhere near where you want to be, you can change this. You can learn how to be happy by just accepting your present, by going with the flow, rather than against it. When you're in the flow of life, everything positive comes your way.

To get into the flow of life you need to become positive by observing positive things in your current reality. You're where you are, but you always have the option to choose where your attention is going to be. You're in complete control of your focus, so you should use it wisely and pay attention to what makes you happy and then focus on this reality. Having once been 100% paralyzed, I can now make myself happy just by focusing on my ability to walk, breathe, and laugh.

Be happy for everything you have in life. This way you'll start appreciating your current reality because your attention will always be fixed on the good aspects of your life. The bad thoughts will die off because you will not pay any attention to them. Feed only the "white dog."

The less you pay attention to the negative aspects of your reality, the less they resonate with you, and with time you will be unable to recognize them at all. Your life will only resonate with good vibes as the bad vibes will drift away.

Once you learn to do this, you'll learn to appreciate where you are in life. It's this appreciation of your current reality that will open the doors to a better reality. It's impossible to hate your present reality and be able to get out of it into a better one. You must embrace your present and remember it's not your future, that's why we set goals and daily state our affirmations.

A store owner was tacking a sign above his door that read "Puppies For Sale." Signs like that have a way of attracting small children, and sure enough, a little boy appeared under the store owner's sign. *"How much are you going to sell the puppies for?"* he asked.

The store owner replied, *"Anywhere from $30 to $50."*

The little boy reached in his pocket and pulled out some change. *"I have $2.37,"* he said. *"Can I please look at them?"*

The store owner smiled and whistled and out of the kennel came Lady, who ran down the aisle of his store followed by five teeny, tiny balls of fur.

One puppy was lagging considerably behind. Immediately the little boy singled out the lagging, limping puppy and said, *"What's wrong with that little dog?"*

The store owner explained that the veterinarian had examined the little puppy and had discovered it didn't have a hip socket. It would always limp. It would always be lame.

The little boy became excited. "That's the puppy I want to buy."

The store owner said, *"No, you don't want to buy that little dog. If you really want him, I'll just give him to you."*

The little boy got quite upset. He looked straight into the store owner's eyes, pointing his finger, and said, *"I don't want you to give him to me. That little dog is worth every bit as much as all the other dogs and I'll pay full price. In fact, I'll give you $2.37 now, and 50 cents a month until I have him paid for."*

The store owner countered, *"You really don't want to buy this little dog. He is never going to be able to run and jump and play with you like the other puppies."*

To his surprise, the little boy reached down and rolled up his pant leg to reveal a badly twisted, crippled left leg supported by a big metal brace. He looked up at the store owner and softly replied, *"Well, I don't run so well myself, and the little puppy will need someone who understands."*

In life, we *ALL* need someone who understands!

When you appreciate where you are and hope to get more, you're allowing all the good things to become part of your reality. When you're negative about your ability to change circumstances and get out of your unsatisfying present reality, you close the doors to the happiness in your future. Remember, there is no better time than now and no better day than today. The Kabbalah teaches us to live each day as if it's our last. Enjoy the moment.

Doubtfulness and other negative feelings and thoughts block you from improving your life. Hopefulness, faith, and happiness open the doors for all your desires to come into your reality.

Relax and let the flow of life take care of you. You'll notice that the more relaxed you get, the less negativity you take on, and the more good things that will come your way. The more days you're happy and relaxed, the more in the flow of life you get, the more of your intentions manifest straight away, and you finally understand how to be happy.

Think and focus more on the great things you want to experience. Taking action in your present will guide you into your future. Never ever feel guilty about who you are or what you've done. What is done is done. You can't relive the past, but you can change the future. Guilt will block you from reaching your goals and desires. Just trust that the universe will sort everything out for you.

There are natural laws that exist internally as well as externally. I commit "5 minutes" every day to bring myself into balance with natural laws, creating a synergy between the internal and the external. By controlling these natural laws, we can increase the quality of our life, the importance of our position, the harmony of our workplace. We will be able to increase our productivity and develop an inner peace. I am not talking of an external law, such as the law of gravity; we don't need to jump off a building to know that a law exists. We only need to abide by it, not defy it.

He lives long that lives well, and time misspent is not lived but lost.

Thomas Fuller

Chapter 16

The Bandits of Time

In my first book, *Lifestyle of the Fit and Famous*, I discuss in detail how utilizing vitamin therapy and mind techniques can alter your genetic structure and your genetic quality. In my previous book, *Dying to Be Young*, I wrote a specific chapter on *youthful aging*. After almost losing my life to get rid of wrinkles, I came to realize it's okay to age, but I also learned we can age gracefully and look good naturally. I go into this in detail at the end of this book in Chapter 37: Turning Back the Clock.

The body consists of a trillion cells that reproduce themselves on an annual basis. These laws of physiology exist whether we accept them or not, and they will exert their presence on us whether we are aware or unaware. The laws of nature are universal and constant, 24 hours a day, 7 days a week, 365 days a year. We live in a busy world governed by laws, natural and unnatural, and as the population of our world continues to grow, the production and demand for technology will continue to grow. It's because of this increase in population, which demands an increase in production, which is fueled by an increase in technology, that we must adapt to the needs of man and woman in order to survive. Time will not stop for us.

In the movie *Wall Street*, Gordon Gecco says, "Money never sleeps," because as we are sleeping in our time zone, the stock market has opened in Japan and people are already trading. The world is always awake someplace at some time. Sleep is a necessity, but to some of us it has become more of a means of escapism. Time controls our lives whether we like it or not. People that don't find time to be healthy, always find time to get sick.

As the sun rises and the sun sets, our life is controlled and coordinated by time. Our day consists of 86,400 seconds. How to utilize this time is our choice. It truly demonstrates the age-old creed that all men are created equal. All men and all women share the same amount of time. They have the same opportunity in every given day; it's a matter of how they utilize their time. By utilizing and implementing time, we can increase production, which will produce higher levels of fulfillment and self-esteem.

In order to use my program, get up "5 minutes" earlier each day and stay up "5 minutes" later. Spend those 10 minutes each day understanding the laws of nature and implementing the new powers you've gained. Everyone's lives are dictated by time. How often do you hear yourself say in the course of a day, *"I would like to write a book, but I don't have time. I would like to develop a better relationship with my spouse, but I don't have time. I would like to exercise, but I don't have time."* Remember, people who don't find time to be healthy always find time to be sick. The paradox of life is that time can work for us or against us. But, time is an age-old excuse. How often do you say to a person, *"We should meet for dinner,"* and they reply, *"I'd love to, but I don't have the time."* They have the same amount of time you do. What they are responding with is, *"It's not my priority to have dinner with you."* They have chosen to utilize their time in another manner, whether more productive or less productive. Internalize their answer. Recognize that you were going to share your time with their time. This is an equal swap.

In any event, you do have the choice. If you are unhappy with your job, you choose to be. If you are unhappy with your relationship, you choose to be. If you are unhappy with your body, you choose to be. Today's world is filled with diet books, exercise media, and gymnasiums that can offer you the ability to raise your level of life. In every activity that you do, there are three questions that you have to ask yourself: *Why am I here? Is this the best utilization of my time? Could my time be utilized better any place else?*

Those three questions, when monitored on a daily basis, which will take 15 seconds of your day, can alter your destiny alone. Why are you here at this moment? You have decided to grow. You have decided that if you can change your life in "5 minutes" a day, you choose to do so. Is this the best utilization of your time? If you look at it on not a micro level, but on a macro level, you will see that the time that you spend now—"5 minutes" a day—can influence the other 23 hours and 55 minutes. There is not time wasted.

In my previous book, *Dying to Be Young*, I share the rules to live your life by. There are no mistakes in life; there are only lessons. You will repeat these lessons until they are learned. In essence, the universal law of time says that you control your life by controlling your time. Time does not control your destiny; it just unfolds it. You control your time, which, when acted on as opposed to reacted to, will produce for you the fulfillment that you are looking for—inner peace and the life of your dreams.

There is a story of four candles by an unknown author.

The four candles burned slowly and their ambiance was so soft you could hear them speak...

The first candle said, "*I Am Peace, but these days, nobody wants to keep me lit.*" Then Peace's flame slowly diminishes and goes out completely.

The second candle said, "*I Am Faith, but these days, I am no longer indispensable.*" Then Faith's flame slowly diminished and went out completely.

The third candle spoke with sadness, "*I Am Love and I haven't the strength to stay lit any longer. People put me aside and don't understand my importance. They even forget to love those who are nearest to them.*" And waiting no longer, Love went out completely.

Suddenly, a child entered the room and saw the three candles no longer burning. The child begins to cry, *"Why are you not burning? You're supposed to stay lit until the end."*

Then the fourth candle spoke gently to the little boy, *"Don't be afraid, for I Am Hope, and while I still burn, we can re-light the other candles."*

With shining eyes the child took the candle of Hope and lit the other three candles.

With the candle of Hope we can bring Peace, Faith, and Love back in our lives.

Have you ever looked in the mirror and said to yourself, *"My life is out of control"*? Your life is never out of control. You are always in control. What you are saying is, *"I have no management, no coordination of my time."* We are controlled by events. Time has developed dominion over us. We no longer have dominion over time, and when time controls us, time can control our very existence. The key is to never give up HOPE— no matter how difficult you may think things are and no matter what the event in life you may be facing.

In life there are two types of events: those that we can control and those that we cannot. Some events that we do not have control over are the changing of seasons, when the sun rises, when the sun sets, when it's high tide, and when it's low tide. But we do have control over our mind-set, and our mind-set controls our attitude. Zig Ziglar says, *"Your attitude, not your aptitude, will determine your altitude."* You can go as high as you want in this world. If you cannot control the event, if you cannot control the season, then control your attitude and adapt to your environment. Without the ability to adapt, you will bring on stress and frustration. An inability to control an event can create significant depression. When you realize that you can control your attitude in the course of any event, then you realize that you can control your destiny.

In life, there is one thing over which you have assured control— yourself. You may not be able to control the events of life, you may not be able to control the events of others, but you are granted absolute control of yourself when you recognize absolute power.

Psychologist Nathaniel L. Brandon, author of *The Psychology of Self-Esteem*, pointed out the direct relationship between self-esteem and productive work. In essence, Brandon's statement was, *"The better you feel about yourself, the more productive you'll be and the more productive you are, the better you'll feel about yourself."*

Recognize that attitude and self-esteem have a direct relationship to productivity. Productivity has a direct relationship to attitude and self-esteem. When you recognize that you have the ability, not to alter time, but to alter your destiny, you become not the passenger, but the driver, and you can steer your course to a higher level of productivity. If you are feeling bad about yourself mentally, then dig in harder physically. Develop a purpose. Be a better parent. Be a better employee. Be more productive and your self-esteem, inner confidence, and inner peace will soar.

One of the biggest fallacies associated with time is that we can save time. You can't save time. You can't accumulate time. You can only utilize the time that is given to you. We all share 86,400 seconds a day. You can alter your life. You can alter your destiny and control your time by giving "5 minutes" or 300 seconds a day to follow your inner master motivator, and you'll still have 86,100 seconds to spare.

A pessimist sees the difficulty in every opportunity; an optimist sees the opportunity in every difficulty.

Winston Churchill

Chapter 17

Opportunity Knocks, It Doesn't Push Down the Door

What are your goals for today? Is there anything that would prevent you from accomplishing them? Of the 6 billion people or so people who currently inhabit the earth, of all the billions of people who have ever lived, there never has been, nor will there ever be, another you. You are even more unique than all of Rembrandt's or Vincent Van Gogh's paintings combined because you are the rarest, most precious commodity you'll ever own. How many times have opportunities been presented to you, but you were scared to take action?

The enemy of opportunity is procrastination. J.G. Holland said, *"God gives every man his food, he just doesn't put it in his nest."*

There are three types of people in this universe:
Those who make things happen.
Those who watch things happen.
Those who say, "What happened?"

If you are one of those people who say, *"What happened?"*, then obviously opportunity has been knocking on your door. You just never let it in for fear of retribution. Fear is not bad. Fear is good. Fear is a master motivator. Fear is what gets us out of bed in the morning—fear

111

we might lose our house, fear we might not be able to pay our bills, or fear of what our friends will say. The paradox is that fear can always undermine, demoralize, and destroy.

An acronym for fear is:

Fₐₗₛₑ

Eᵥᵢdₑₙcₑ (experience)

Aₚₚₑₐᵣᵢₙg

Rₑₐₗ

It was determined at Harvard University that more than 90% of our fears will never materialize. Yet, that 90% of fear can block us from our 10% of opportunity. Fear comes in two different levels: conscious and subconscious.

Conscious fear is the fear we feel when the teacher asks us to hand in a report, the boss asks us for completion of our assignment, or it's time to go on Space Mountain at Disney World. Subconscious fears are the fears that we have harbored throughout our lives and block us from moving ahead. Our past fears should not determine our future victories. Recognize that many of our fears have been pushed into the back of our brain, hoping that they will never surface, and not recognizing that these fears actually surface daily. In essence, they are always there, we just may not be conscious of them.

When my wife and I were 100% paralyzed, we were scared. Our lives were inundated with fears. My wife still gets nightmares. But we had to conquer our fears. I was scared when it was time to take me off the ventilator. For 50-plus years I breathed on my own; now I was scared my body would forget how to do something we do so naturally. I had to look fear and the ventilator in the eye and defeat them—not physically, but mentally. I kept telling the doctors that I needed one more day, one more week. I wanted time to overcome my fear, but you must overcome your fears and not allow time to be your excuse.

Fear is the father of procrastination. It's fear that makes us procrastinate in opening the door. Many people fear speaking in front of audiences. Winston Churchill stuttered when he was young. He overcame this problem by recognizing his weakness. He developed knowledge, which granted him power, which improved his productivity, which then led him to higher levels of confidence and self-esteem. Churchill became an accomplished, charismatic speaker who would be remembered not as a stutterer, but as a world leader and an author of history.

Winston Churchill once wrote, *"Courage is rightly considered the foremost of virtues, for upon it, all others depend."* Fear is, and always has been, the greatest enemy of mankind.

When Franklin D. Roosevelt said, *"The only thing we have to fear is fear itself,"* he was saying that the emotion of fear, rather than the reality of what we fear, is the cause of the associated anxiety, stress, and unhappiness. When we develop the habit of courage and unshakable self-confidence, a whole new world of possibilities opens up to us. What would you dare to dream, be, or do if you weren't afraid of anything in the whole world?

What we need to learn from the great leaders of our nations is that the habit of courage can be learned, just as any other skill can be learned. However, to do this we need to go to work systematically to diminish and eradicate our fears, while simultaneously building the kind of courage that will enable us to deal fearlessly with the inevitable ups and downs of life. We need to spend "5 minutes" each day attacking our fears. Write them down on a piece of paper, look them in the eye, and work on removing the fears that are holding you back.

The starting point in overcoming fear and developing courage is to look at the factors that predispose us toward fear. Syndicated columnist Ann Landers wrote, *"If I were asked to give what I considered the single most useful bit of advice for all humanity, it would be this: Expect trouble as an inevitable part of life, and when it comes, hold your head high. Look it squarely in the eye and say, 'I will be bigger than you. You cannot defeat me.'"*

This is the kind of attitude that leads to victory.

For many of us, the root of all fear was our childhood conditioning. Modern science has yet to come close to developing a computer as complex and creative as the human brain. As the owner of this magnificent biomachine, it's our responsibility to program it. All too often, though, we hand over the job to others, we make ourselves victims of circumstances. Once again, say you begin the day in a great state of mind and then your car won't start. Or you get to work and your assistant or key co-worker calls in sick. Or the boss is in a bad mood and yells at you. By the end of the day you've been reprogrammed—and the program has plenty of bugs in it.

This is when you have to remember to take charge and say, "I will greet every obstacle, every fear head on, face to face. I will turn each obstacle into a challenge, and each challenge into a success."

This is not always easy to do given the beliefs many of us were weaned on. The root source of fear for many of us is our childhood conditioning that causes us to experience two types of fear:

The fear of failure, which causes us to think,
I can't, I can't, I can't.

The fear of rejection, which causes us to think,
I have to, I have to, I have to.

Based on those fears, we become preoccupied with the idea of losing our money, our time, and our emotional investment in a relationship. We become hypersensitive to the opinions and possible criticisms of others, sometimes to the point where we are afraid to do anything that anyone else might disapprove of. Our fears tend to paralyze us, holding us back from taking constructive action in the direction of our dreams and goals. Fear is the enemy of opportunity. We hesitate, we become indecisive, and we procrastinate; we make excuses and find reasons not to move ahead. And finally, we feel frustrated, caught in the double bind of, *"I have to, but I can't."*

I, like many of you, was raised on these clichés. I was too young to see the inherent flaws, too dependent on the good will of the adults around me to challenge their beliefs. In time, I learned to let go of these limiting thoughts and you can do the same.

How many of us were raised in a totally positive environment? How often did we hear that we could do whatever we wanted and be the person we dreamed of being? If you didn't hear this very often, start telling it to yourself. Regardless of how much negative programming you were subjected to, you have the ability to change to overcome any and all fears.

Fear is often caused by ignorance. When we have limited information, we tend to be tense and insecure about the outcome of our actions. Ignorance causes us to fear change, to fear the unknown, and limits our confidence to try anything new or different. The key to this formula, this mindset, is that the reverse is also true. The very act of gathering more and more information about any particular subject or situation allows us to be more confident and courageous in that area. There are parts of our life when we have no fear at all because we feel knowledgeable and capable of handling whatever happens. As a chiropractor, you can put anyone's neck in my hands and my confidence destroys any fear of hurting the patient. However, give me a three-foot putt for five dollars with either of my friends Bill Meyer, Pete or Andy Brock, Warren Zwecker, Joe Jillson, Harold Rosen, Joe Littenberg, Rich Kaufman, John Preston or Richard Paladino and those same confident hands begin to shake. It's then that I dig deep to focus and remove those demons from mind, my spirit.

Once you've recognized the factors that can cause fear, the second step in overcoming it is to sit down and take the time to objectively define and analyze your own fears. At the top of a sheet of paper, write down the question, *"What am I afraid of?"*

I have learned in life that most people are afraid of something. It's normal and natural to be concerned about your physical, emotional, and financial survival. The courageous person is not a person who is unafraid.

As Mark Twain said, *"Courage is resistance to fear, mastery of fear—not absence of fear."*

It's not whether or not you are afraid. We're all afraid. The question is how do you deal with the fear? The courageous person is simply one who goes forward in spite of the fear.

There are two types of changes we are concerned with. The first is physical change, to which most of you reading this book are already committed. The second, more subtle change is psychological. It involves shifting our attitudes and releasing our fears, doubts, worries, anxieties, and insecurities. I define "average" as *"the best of the worst and the worst of the best."* Are you willing to settle for being average?

The future belongs to the risk takers, not the security seekers. Life is perverse in the sense that the more you seek security, the less of it you have. But the more you seek opportunity, the more likely it is that you will achieve the security that you desire.

The first and perhaps most important kind of courage is the courage to begin, to launch, and to step out in faith. This is the courage to try something new or different, to move out of your comfort zone, with no guarantee of success.

If opportunity knocks, take a risk and open the door, or better yet make your own opportunities.

By many people's standards Abraham Lincoln was considered by many to be ugly. There is a story that one day a man came up to Abraham Lincoln, put a gun up to his head, and said, *"I swore if I ever met a man who was uglier than I was, I would shoot him right there on the spot."*

Abraham Lincoln, in his calm, confident, tranquil manner, looked at this man and replied, *"Sir, if I am as ugly as you, go ahead and pull the trigger."*

Both men then laughed. Abraham Lincoln did not face fear at that moment; he faced an opportunity to overcome a fear with a greater inner strength, greater self-esteem, and unparalleled productivity.

Chapter 17

Every day we should spend "5 minutes" seeing what opportunities are out there for us and taking action. Every day we should open a new door, a new opportunity. This may be in the form of meeting someone new, giving someone a compliment, or just helping someone else. Once we identify the many opportunities in our lives we can open the doors to our success.

It is easier to prevent bad habits than to break them.

Benjamin Franklin

Chapter 18

The Power of Habit

We are all creatures of habit, whether we like it or not. Our lives are patterned by habits. The option that we have is the type of habits we develop: good habits or bad habits. Habits are reflected by the individual's psychological and physiological requirements; they begin psychologically and often become physiological. Take cigarettes, for example. No one is born with a physiological need for nicotine, but psychologically we determine that the reward of smoking is greater than the fear of smoking. Therefore, the habit is initially psychological, whether it's to look older or impress our friends, and then becomes physiological. Obesity is another example. Most people eat based upon desire, rather than physical necessity. Ninety-nine percent of human beings are not born overweight. We must understand that in order to be happy or develop inner peace, we have psychological requirements. These psychological requirements help to develop or expose our habits.

I don't think that anybody can question the need to live. We can see it in newborns who overcome unbelievable obstacles to maintain life. Without the ability to communicate, they develop the ability to attract attention and psychologically impose their will upon those around them. The elderly also maintain a strong desire to live. Many people whose friends have already been visited by the white cloud of death continue to go on, masterfully motivating their lives. The elderly set a strong precedent in resisting the pull of death despite physical or psychological handicaps.

It's the most powerful of all innate instincts that, upon facing danger, we are able to reach limits never before recognized. It's my recommendation that we devote our lives to developing the ability to live while maintaining inner peace. We must devote "5 minutes" a day toward mental preparation. A ball player does not go on a field without warming up. Yet, many of us wake up in the morning, jump out of bed, throw down a cup of coffee, jump in the car, and get on the phone without a pause. Research indicates that the average American no longer even takes lunch. He alters his lunch habit based upon a psychological need to succeed, even if his physiological needs are not satisfied.

The desire to succeed maintains itself in our occupation, our relationship, and in loving or being loved. We must not languish in our past. The greatest master motivator in the world is love—giving love and being loved. An inability to love or be loved may have devastating results, because it's love that is our main internal motivator. We must love what we are doing in order to be more productive. By being more productive we become more powerful and we create higher self-esteem. This will create more endorphins. Endorphins are the internal substances that give the body a euphoric feeling. It can be accomplished by exercising, but it may also be accomplished by laughing. It may also be acquired by loving. Endorphins have the power and potential to alter the brain in the same manner as morphine. Why do we live in a world that is devoured by drug addiction and crimes related to this very drug addiction? Is it a lack of discipline or is it simply a lack of love? If love is not in your life, then you are empty. You are in a canoe without a paddle. Being loved gives us a level of self-esteem, a level of importance, and lets us feel unique. It recognizes our purpose

There was a man taking a morning walk at the beach. He saw that along with the morning tide came hundreds of starfish and when the tide receded, they were left behind and with the morning sun rays, they would die. The tide was fresh and the starfish were alive. The man took a few steps, picked one and threw it into the water. He did that repeatedly.

Right behind him there was another person who couldn't understand what this man was doing. He caught up with him and asked, *"What are you doing? There are hundreds of starfish. How many can you help? What difference does it make?"* This man did not reply, took two more steps, picked up another one, threw it into the water, and said, **"It makes a difference to this one."**

What difference are you making in this world? Why not develop a winning habit of making people happy, making yourself happy. Imagine if everyone made a small difference, we'd end up with a big difference, wouldn't we?

Our lives are consumed by a variety of habits, both good and bad. We need to develop healthy habits, happy habits, and successful habits. As discussed earlier, Dr. Maxwell Maltz, author of *Psycho-Cybernetics*, said that if you do something for 21 consecutive days it becomes a habit. Many mornings I get up in my home in Florida and I go out to run. It's hot, it's humid, and often running is not fun. But, because of the endorphin rush that I feel, it has become a healthy habit that I feel compelled to do upon waking. It has become more than a psychological need. It was psychologically induced, but it's now almost a physiological need. My innate structure motivates my brain to get my backside out of bed and to start running. For the past 14 years, my recently deceased Dalmatian was my inspiration. She loved our daily runs and made me feel guilty if I wanted to skip even one day. She would start our morning by staring at me and became my jogging buddy. It's amazing, but a dog is truly "man's best friend." If you want to diet, do it with someone. If you want to exercise, do it with someone. If you don't have the power to do it on your own, then don't do it alone. Find a partner.

Habits are many times predetermined by our needs. Habits can be altered by our desire to live, our desire to love, our desire for the need of variety, and our desire to be healthy. We must implement healthy habits in our lives.

Spend "5 minutes" a day mapping out your daily program. I will never forget the scene in the Disney movie, *Alice in Wonderland*, when Alice confronts the Cheshire cat and asks, *"Which road do I take?"* The cat answers Alice, *"Where are you going?"* and Alice responds, *"I don't know,"* to which the cat says, *"Then it doesn't matter which road you take."* If you don't know where you are going, then that is where you will end up. Set goals and monitor them. Setting goals is a healthy habit. Monitoring goals is a healthier habit. If you spent "5 minutes" per day setting goals and monitoring the goals you set, you will reach levels of health, wealth, and happiness beyond your current state. If you don't plan to succeed, then you don't have a plan for success. If you don't plan to be healthy, then you don't have a healthy plan. If you don't plan to be happy, then you might as well plan not to be happy. We must plan our life and live our plan.

When you recognize that setting goals is a healthy habit, then you must affirm them, and again, we revisit the word "affirmation." We must say who we are, what we are, and where we are going. "I am happy, I am healthy, and I am successful." Life is for living, loving, laughing, and learning, not just for whining, worrying, or working. We need to live, we need to love, we need to laugh, and these can all be healthy habits.

Norman Cousins, in his book, *Anatomy of An Illness*, showed how laughing, when coordinated with nutrition, overcame terminal illness. Don't diminish the power of the brain. We have the psychological ability to alter our physiological state. When we recognize that power and introduce that power into habit, then we are developing the habits of success. We must develop proper habits for activities of daily living. These habits determine the way we sleep and the time that we sleep. In essence, all that I ask you to do is to get up "5 minutes" earlier and stay up "5 minutes" a day later. Use the "5 minutes" at night to plan what you are going to do the next day, and utilize the "5 minutes" the next morning to chart out your daily plan. If you stretch and exercise during those "5 minutes," then you will develop a healthy habit by introducing that activity for 30 days. Let's develop the "5 minute" habit. Let's make a habit of setting goals, saying our affirmations, and working on our attitude. Let your goals create a roadmap, a beacon by which to guide your life. Do not be a ship without navigation lights.

Change your habits and you can change your life.

Meyer Kaplan

Chapter 19

Healthy Habits

Many people take a coffee break. The average American consumes 400 mg of caffeine a day. An excess of 200 mg of caffeine a day is considered addicting by many experts. Many of us are addicted to caffeine, a substance that increases our heart rate and is a vasodilator, yet we wonder why we are a country devoured by anxiety attacks. We are pushing our system, not only psychologically, but also physiologically, by chemical dependency to a state, not of inner peace, but of excitement. We must develop a habit of drinking natural, herbal teas. Now, am I saying to eliminate coffee? No. What I am saying is to eliminate the excess. Instead of taking a coffee break, take a meditation break, a breathing break, and in this breathing break you should follow a 3-2-1 formula.

"5 Minute" Breathing Break

Every day, when you are in the office, take "5 minutes," get in a comfortable position, and take a deep breath in through your nose, taking in all the air you can to the count of three. As you take in this breath you should feel your stomach expand. If your stomach is not expanding as you take in this breath, you are not breathing properly. As you feel your stomach and chest expand, hold this breath for two seconds and then let it out quickly. After you do this exercise for one minute, take the next minute to sit there and feel the overall state of relaxation that has overtaken your body. Do this exercise, 3-2-1, one minute on and one minute off.

"5 Minute" Exercise Break

Five minutes a day might not be enough time to put to exercise, but it's a good start. Do pushups or stretch—something is always better than nothing. The key is that once you realize how good it feels to exercise, "5 minutes" will lead to 10 minutes and 10 minutes will lead to 15 minutes. We must learn that the only way to accomplish any large goal is to set smaller goals that bring us to our point of success. People with healthy habits have healthy attitudes.

How do you recognize these people?

Healthy people:

1. Like other people

2. Enjoy life

3. Have fun

4. Want more

5. Have many good friends

6. Compliment others

7. Show appreciation

People with poor habits develop poor attitudes. These people:

1. Don't like people

2. Don't enjoy life

3. Don't have much fun

4. Don't care if they do better or have more

5. Have few friends

6. Don't compliment people

7. Don't show appreciation and seem to complain and condemn more

Some people wake up in the morning and say, *"Good morning, Lord,"* and other people wake up in morning and say, *"Good Lord, morning!"* Which are you?

Set your habits and your attitudes by setting a goal and making an affirmation to spend "5 minutes" a day doing the following mental exercise.

"5 Minute" Mental Exercise

Ask yourself several times throughout the day:

1. What is my attitude on a scale of one to ten? (Attempt to be as close to 10 as you possibly can.)

2. Where do I want to be on an attitude scale of one to ten?

3. Most importantly: What do I need to do to get there?

4. What can I do for myself or what can I do for someone else today?

5. What can I do to make someone else feel good?

6. What can I do to make myself feel good?

7. To whom can I show my love and gratitude today?

Change your attitude and you will change your life. William James, a pioneering father of American psychology, said, *"The greatest discovery of my generation is that man can alter his life by altering his attitude."* An attitude can be determined by habit. Many of us habitually have a poor attitude. We need to recognize our attitude and have a habit of asking ourselves the question, *What is my attitude at this moment?* By developing a habit of challenging your psychological state you can alter your physiological being. Cultivate the habit of laughter and lighten up. Give yourself the permission to have fun. Wallace "Wally" Amos, Jr., the "Famous Amos" chocolate chip cookie guru, would always say, *"It's okay to have fun."* Remember, life is boring for boring people. Learn to have fun with yourself. Learn to have fun with life. Remember the three rules of life:

1. Don't sweat the small stuff.

2. Everything is small stuff.

3. None of us are getting out of life alive.

I give you permission to take life a little lighter. I give you permission to enjoy your life right here and right now. I give you permission to laugh, to smile, and to have fun in your life. If laughter can heal, it can also prevent sickness and disease. Introduce yourself to a person and smile. Watch their reaction. Smiling for someone else will usually bring back a smile to you. People develop the habit of smiling. Many people don't understand the power of laughter and humor. But these two components can be great companions throughout life. If you cannot give yourself permission to laugh and take life a little less seriously and if you feel like you need permission, then please let me give you permission. From this day forth you have permission to lighten up and have fun.

My father used to always say, *"Life is never what it seems—it's always more, better, greater."* Open up your eyes and look around. Life is what you make it. You see, we get what we pay for. One common saying tells us we get back from life whatever we put into life. Life can be wonderful and is wonderful. We reap what we sow. Remember, we are all given 86,400 seconds a day and it's up to us to use these seconds for our good. Hopefully you have learned from my book how "5 minutes"—300 seconds a day—can change your life. By dedicating just 300 seconds, you still have 86,100 seconds left in your day. I am not asking for much, but "5 minutes" a day can give you everything you have ever wanted in life and more.

Where do we begin? We begin with our "5 Minute Habits" of:

1. Goal setting

2. Daily review of goals

3. Affirmations

4. Meditation

5. Exercise

6. Reading or listening to motivational material

If you master the power of habit and spent "5 minutes" on each category above, it would take only 30 minutes per day—that's a small price for big change. That would still leave us with 1,410 minutes a day. Time is often our friend and never our enemy. Time is life and life is time, choose to use your time for good, and then you will have nothing but good times.

Let me share a story with you that my professor Dr. Gutstein once told me.

A group of alumni, highly established in their careers, got together to visit their old university professor. Conversation soon turned into complaints about stress in work and life.

Offering his guests coffee, the professor went to the kitchen and returned with a large pot of coffee and an assortment of cups —porcelain, plastic, glass, crystal, some plain-looking, some expensive, some exquisite—telling them to help themselves to the coffee. When all the students had a cup of coffee in hand, the professor said:

If you noticed, all the nice-looking, expensive cups were taken up, leaving behind the plain and cheap ones. While it is normal for you to want only the best for yourselves, that is the source of your problems and stress. Be assured that the cup itself adds no quality to the coffee. In most cases it's just more expensive and in some cases even hides what we drink. What all of you really wanted was coffee, not the cup, but you consciously went for the best cups. And then you began eyeing each other's cups.

Now consider this: Life is the coffee; while the jobs, money and position in society are the cups. They are just tools to hold and contain Life, and the type of cup we have does not define, nor change, the quality of Life we live. Sometimes, by concentrating only on the cup, we fail to enjoy the coffee God has provided us.

God brews the coffee, not the cups. Enjoy your coffee!

My father used to always say and believe, *"The happiest people don't neccessarily have the best of everything. They just make the best of everything."*

When we wake up in the morning, we are given today to use however we want. It's just a day. It's up to us to make it good or bad, positive or negative. Our decisions make our day what it becomes. We continually have choices and nobody can make choices or decisions for us. People can alter our choices and people can disagree with our decisions, but it's ultimately our choice.

Life is full of decisions from the moment we first wake up in the morning. Our decision is to stay in bed or get out of bed. It's our decision to have a good day or a bad day. It's our decision to eat breakfast or not. It's our decision to go to work or not go to work. It's our decision to stay mad at our spouse and it's also our decision to forgive him or her. Our choices reflect in every part of our day. Do I wear the white shirt? Do I wear the blue shirt? Do I have two cups of coffee? Do I eat the bacon? Do I have the donut? Our day is constantly guided by choices. Of course, some decisions and choices are much harder than others. There are some decisions we would rather not make. There are decisions we must make, no matter how difficult the choices are. But they are ours to make. Life becomes what we make it. Some decisions we confront carry much greater consequences than others, and of course the greater the decision, the greater the consequences. It's important for all of us to realize the choice or decisions we make today will affect our lives tomorrow, because we are where we are today due to the choices that we made 5 or 10 years ago.

Jim Rhon, a motivational speaker, said, *"We know that ten years from now we'll arrive; the major question is—where?"* Our decisions made today will influence the rest of our lives. They can influence our social and economic development. They can influence our family, our career. They can influence our economic state, our physiological state, and our psychological state.

What we do today determines where we are tomorrow. It's up to us to be happy, mad, or sad. We must develop healthy habits. We must embrace life.

You cannot control what happens to you, but you can control your attitude toward what happens to you, and in that, you will be mastering change rather than allowing it to master you.

Brian Tracy

Chapter 20

Comfort Zone

We have now learned that we can alter our habits by altering our attitude. Many times, habits are induced as a physiological state that creates a psychological comfort zone. Comfort zones are easy to get into and hard to escape. A comfort zone is being so comfortable in what you're doing that you aren't striving to do or be or have any more than what you have. A comfort zone may be likened to a grave. A comfort zone is a rut, and a rut is nothing more than a grave with both ends open. A comfort zone is a state of mind. It's a state in which you feel comfortable and don't want to change. The capitol of the state of comfort is habit. Perhaps you developed the habit of sitting and watching television in the evening, maybe going so far as to have your dinner served in front of the television on a tray. This is a habit.

Your comfort zone is doing the same thing the same way. Perhaps your comfort zone is never speaking at meetings or at the office, or if you do speak, you do so from your seat. If you stand up, maybe you feel it will bring too much attention upon yourself. Sometimes we need to step up to step out of our comfort zone. Remember, a comfort zone is governed by habit and habits can be changed by attitude. A comfort zone is where you feel comfortable, a situation you don't want to leave because doing so would make you uncomfortable. What we need to do is get out of our comfort zones and develop health zones. We sometimes need to make ourselves feel a little bit uncomfortable to make a few forward steps. We need to walk before we can run. We have to stretch to stretch our limits by stretching our minds.

Oliver Wendell Holmes said, *"A mind stretched by a new idea will never return to its original dimension."* If you find yourself living and functioning in a comfort zone, you have to make changes in your life. Your comfort zone may be driving to work the same way, eating the same breakfast, or wearing the same color shirt. Take a new way to work, take a new road. Stop at a new place for the newspaper or a different place for a cup of coffee.

Go out to lunch with somebody different. Watch a different channel this evening, a different show. Take a college course, a computer course. Start a new diet or a new exercise program. Spend more time with your family. Do things that are different. If you continue to do the same thing the same way, expect the same results. The only difference between a grave and a rut is its length and depth.

A philosophy professor stood before his class and had some items in front of him. When class began, wordlessly he picked up a large empty mayonnaise jar and proceeded to fill it with rocks, rocks about 2" in diameter.

He then asked the students if the jar was full. They agreed that it was. So the professor then picked up a box of pebbles and poured them into the jar. He shook the jar lightly. The pebbles, of course, rolled into the open areas between the rocks.

He then asked the students again if the jar was full. They agreed it was.

The students laughed. The professor picked up a box of sand and poured it into the jar. Of course, the sand filled up everything else.

"Now," said the professor, *"I want you to recognize that this is your life. The rocks are the important things—your family, your partner, your health, your children—anything that is so important to you that if it were lost, you*

would be nearly destroyed. The pebbles are the other things that matter like your job, your house, your car. The sand is everything else. The small stuff.

"If you put the sand into the jar first, there is no room for the pebbles or the rocks. The same goes for your life. If you spend all your energy and time on the small stuff, you will never have room for the things that are important to you.

"Pay attention to the things that are critical to your happiness. Play with your children. Take time to get medical checkups. Take your partner out dancing. There will always be time to go to work, clean the house, give a dinner party and fix the disposal.

"Take care of the rocks first—the things that really matter. Set your priorities. The rest is just sand."

Let's spend the next "5 minutes" with a healthy habit of studying and incorporating these mental exercises.

"5 Minute" Exercise

1. Do something different every day for the next 30 days, if only for "5 minutes" a day.

2. Think differently about a situation or person you do not like for the next week.

3. See that person or situation in a way that can alter your destiny.

4. Whatever has been comfortable for you—change.

5. Don't stop at anything and you will you finish everything.

One of the most powerful examples relating to comfort zones was signed by Pastor Martin Niemöller at the Council of the Evangelical

Church in Germany, October 18th in 1945.

Declaration of Guilt

> In Germany, the Nazis first came for the communists, and I didn't speak up because I was not a communist.

> Then they came for the Jews, and I did not speak up because I was not a Jew.

> Then they came for the trade unionists, and l did not speak up because I wasn't a trade unionist.

> Then they came for the Catholics, and I was a Protestant; so I didn't speak up.

> Then they came to me; by that time there was no one to speak up for anyone.

Expect a miracle every day, for life is of itself a miracle. Expect to change. Develop healthy habits. Develop positive habits. Develop winning habits because a negative habit will develop guilt, and guilt will develop a poor attitude that will adversely alter our physiological and psychological state.

Remember:

1. *Winners do things that losers don't like to do.*
2. *Winners do things that losers don't find time to do.*
3. *Winners do things that losers don't feel they need to do.*

Make yourself a winner. Make winning a habit. Take that one step further; follow in the great steps of Michael Jordan and make winning a habit. You should accept nothing less.

What you are—is where you want to be.

Where you want to go—is where you will be.

"It's not what you are that holds you back; it's what you think you are not."

We have all heard the cliché, *"You are what you eat."* I believe that, *"You are what you read, watch, and think."* The Biblical affirmation of this in *The Book of Proverbs* reads, *"As he thinketh in his heart, so he is."* Now is the time to get out of your comfort zone. Maybe every night after dinner you immediately sit in front of the television. Tonight, for "5 minutes," do something different. Take a walk, read a story, meditate, develop your goals for tomorrow, or just give thanks to God for giving you another day of life

My father once told me the story of the prolific baseball scout who was being honored upon his retirement. One reporter in his forthright, yet brash manner, asked the scout on his day of glory, *"Isn't it true that you watched Ty Cobb play and didn't feel he had what it takes."* He answered, *"I saw Ty Cobb play when he was 18 years old. He was good, but not great. He entered the major leagues at the age of 21. Somewhere between the ages of 18 and 21, Ty Cobb decided to pay the price that took him from goodness to greatness."*

Each of us has this ability within us. James Baldwin wrote, *"Not everything that is faced can be changed, but nothing can be changed until it's faced."*

Sophocles said, *"Heaven never helps the man who will not act."*

Now is your time to act. Accept your infinite uniqueness and reach out and do something different. Once you leave your comfort zone you're able to explore its potential and share its power among your peers. Each of us has senses that guide us through the day, but most of us rely only on what we see. Maybe we need to listen more and develop our sense of hearing. By listening we can help others. Ask someone if there was one thing about you they would change, what would it be? Now spend "5 minutes" each day to change this flaw or any flaw. Let's not just stay where we are, let's grow and let's grow together. In order to grow we must learn who we are and how we're seen in the eyes of others. Self-observation and evaluation is often not comfortable and to learn these lessons you begin by listening.

Chapter 20

Listen

Take a moment to listen today,
To what your friends and family are trying to say.
Listen today whatever you do,
Or they will not be there to listen to you.
Listen to their problems and listen to their needs,
Praise their smallest triumphs and their smallest deeds.
Listen to their complaints, their chatter of pain,
Offer them your love, without thinking of gain.
Listen to your family,
Keep your priorities in sight,
For your family will nourish your soul and make
You shine in the night.
Take a moment to listen today,
To what your co-workers, family, and friends are trying to say.
Listen today, whatever you do,
For then they will come back and listen to you.

Author Unknown

Spend "5 minutes" today listening to your children, your parents, your relatives, your friends. Remember, there is a big difference between hearing and listening. Hearing lets us know the music is playing, but listening lets us know what the music is saying. Spend "5 minutes" a day listening to those you love, those you care about, and I assure you when you need someone to listen to you, they'll be happy to return the favor. It only takes "5 minutes" to make a difference in someone's life, even your own. If you want a better life, you must move out of your comfort zone. The best way to leave your comfort zone is to stop focusing on yourself and start focusing on helping and leading others.

Lead yourself out of your comfort zone and lead others to their potential. When you stop focusing on yourself and start focusing on helping and leading others you will enter the spiritual zone, a zone that will deliver to you the inner peace you desire. This is no easy task—to stop focusing on yourself, to focus on others, to lead others—but if you have invested your "5 minutes" daily, now is your time to make a difference. Remember, *"If you want to lead the band, you have to face the music."* The music in your heart is now telling you to take action in your life, to lead yourself and your family by example. My goal today, the purpose of this chapter is for you to take action, to lead you out of your comfort zone. By leaving your comfort zone you begin to lead by example. Now is your turn to make a difference. Here are the traits of a good leader. Spend "5 minutes" today and develop the habits and traits of leaders.

"5 Minute" Traits of a Good Leader

1. **Honest** — Display sincerity, integrity, and candor in all your actions. Deceptive behavior will not inspire trust.

2. **Competent** — Base your actions on reason and moral principles. Do not make decisions based on childlike emotional desires or feelings.

3. **Forward-looking** — Set goals and have a vision of the future. The vision must be owned throughout the organization. Effective leaders envision what they want and how to get it. They habitually pick priorities stemming from their basic values.

4. **Inspiring** — Display confidence in all that you do. By showing endurance in mental, physical, and spiritual stamina, you will inspire others to reach for new heights. Take charge when necessary.

5. **Intelligent** — Read, study, and seek challenging assignments.

6. **Fair-minded** — Show fair treatment to all people. Prejudice is the enemy of justice. Display empathy by being sensitive to the feelings, values, interests, and well-being of others.

7. **Broad-minded** — Seek out diversity.

8. **Courageous** — Have the perseverance to accomplish a goal, regardless of the seemingly insurmountable obstacles. Display a confident calmness when under stress.

9. **Straightforward** — Use sound judgment to make a good decisions at the right time.

10. **Imaginative** — Make timely and appropriate changes in your thinking, plans, and methods. Show creativity by thinking of new and better goals, ideas, and solutions to problems. Be innovative!

Compiled by the Santa Clara University and the Tom Peters Group.

General Patton said, *"Lead, follow, or get out of the way."*
Be a leader.

A man in debt is so far a slave.

Ralph Waldo Emerson

Chapter 21

Life After Debt

We all know the story of the greedy king named Midas. He had a lot of gold and the more he had the more he wanted. He stored all the gold in his vaults and used to spend time every day counting it.

One day while he was counting a stranger came from nowhere and said he would grant him a wish. The king was delighted and said, *"I would like everything I touch to turn to gold."* The stranger asked the king, *"Are you sure?"* The king replied, *"Yes."* So the stranger said, *"Starting tomorrow morning with the sun rays you will get the golden touch."* The king thought he must be dreaming, this couldn't be true. But the next day when he woke up, he touched the bed, his clothes—everything turned to gold. He looked out of the window and saw his daughter playing in the garden. He decided to give her a surprise and thought she would be happy. But before he went to the garden he decided to read a book. The moment he touched it, it turned into gold and he couldn't read it. Then he sat to have breakfast and the moment he touched the fruit and the glass of water, they turned to gold. He was getting hungry and he said to himself, *I can't eat and drink gold.* Just about that time his daughter came running and he hugged her and she turned into a gold statue. There were no more smiles left.

The king bowed his head and started crying. The stranger who gave the wish came again and asked the king if he was happy with his golden touch. The king said he was the most miserable man. The stranger asked,

"What would you rather have, your food and loving daughter or lumps of gold and her golden statue?" The king cried and asked for forgiveness. He said, *"I will give up all my gold. Please give me my daughter back because without her I have lost everything worth having."* The stranger said to the king, *"You have become wiser than before,"* and he reversed the spell. He got his daughter back in his arms and the king learned a lesson that he never forget for the rest of his life.

It is good to aspire to be successful; in fact, I recommend it. But as Midas proved, there are more important things in life then money. Unlike the game of basketball where players can be substituted, the game of life allows no substitutions or replays. We may not get a second chance to reverse our tragedies as the king did. The key to financial success is to not be greedy and avoid debt.

Most people, young and old, seem to get themselves into debt at some time. This chapter deals with how to get out of debt, stay out of debt, and even accumulate wealth. One excellent book on the subject is *The Wealthy Barber*. Another excellent book is by Todd Barnhardt, *The Five Rituals of Wealth*. (For more books from Dr. Kaplan's Recommended Reading list, go to www.5minutemotivator.com.)

In order to succeed monetarily, we must understand the power and influence that money has over our lives. Money is a master motivator.

We must first discuss those who are in debt. How did they develop that trait? Very simply—they spent more than they earned. There are, however, many people who haven't yet reached that state in their lives. How does one get out of debt? One way to get out of debt is to never get into it. Of all the books I've read, one of the best is George Claussen's book, *The Richest Man in Babylon*. In this book, George Claussen develops one simple rule: *The easiest way out of debt is not to spend more than you make.*

The first rule of money is to pay yourself first. When you get your paycheck, take your own percentage first, whether 10% or 40%. Most people say, *"Well, that's common sense."* But actually, the average person deposits their check and then pays everybody before they pay themselves. They pay their house payment or rent, their utility bills, their car loan, their insurance premiums. Then they go out and shop for food, they buy a new outfit and keep whatever is left over. The problem is that sometimes in that month there is nothing left over. At the end of certain months you don't have enough in your paycheck to pay yourself.

What you should do is take whatever amount of money you feel you can live without. (A Biblical number is a 10% tithe of our earnings.) In *The Wealthy Barber*, the author elaborates on the 10% principle. By removing 10% of your paycheck, most people will not even miss it, no matter how great a number it sounds. You should take that 10% and invest it. You can start by putting your money into a savings account, mutual funds, tax-free bonds, real estate, or the stock market. You must determine which yield you want. The lower the risk, the lower the yield; the higher the risk, the higher the yield. I am not here to give you investment advice and whatever decision you make is your own. But what I would like to recommend is that you develop a habit of money management, that you develop a habit of paying yourself first (saving for the future) and then paying the world (your bills).

By increasing your net worth you will increase your confidence. Once again, you'll be developing a positive habit. You will develop a productive habit that will increase your self-esteem. As this money grows and accumulates in interest or profits, you don't spend that profit. One thing I was taught, that the wealthy will teach their own children and that I have taught my own children, is never spend your principle. There is an old story that in times past the wealthy used to wake their children in the middle of the night and demand, *"What is the number one rule of money?"* The number one rule is never spending your principle. You can only spend or reinvest your interest. Therefore, you can never have less than you have accumulated, you can only have more. It should be your goal to live on the profit of your investments, and the way you can do that is to start saving money—no matter how little—and save it regularly. Pay yourself first. An easy way to accumulate money is to take the word "spend" out of your vocabulary. Remember, we don't spend money. When you think about spending, it's gone. What you are doing with money is using or giving money. That way, it's not gone. It will come back to you in a greater amount.

For those of you who are in debt, there are many ways to get out of debt. There are professional clinics, counselors, and money managers who can assist you. Some people who are not in a great amount of debt do not even realize that they are in debt. One way to find out is to do a financial analysis. Review all your credit cards. Are they paid in full? Is there debt? Do you have student loans? That is also a debt. Do you have a mortgage on your home? That is debt. Whenever you have a systematized monthly payment, it's a debt. You must look to pay down your debt by increasing your principle payment. By doubling your mortgage payments on a 30-year mortgage, you can pay for your home in 7 years. There are principles of money. There are laws of finance. These are all natural laws and you need to follow them. Seek out advice and guidance. Every law of debt begins with your paycheck. When you get your paycheck, spend "5 minutes" doing the following. First, divide it into three portions and pay yourself 10%. Again, you will take that portion and put it away. Next, take 70% to pay your covered living expenses, and take the remaining 20% and divide it up: 10% to pay for outstanding bills and debts and 10% to put into a savings. You must live on 10%, pay 10% towards your debt, and invest 10% towards your future. By investing "5 minutes" per paycheck into this formula you will open the doors to financial freedom.

Once we develop good money habits, we will learn there is life after debt. Often, you can make arrangements with your creditors or set up a budget that allows you to live on 70% of your earnings.

Whether you are in debt or not, you can achieve success and prosperity all the more quickly by following simple formulas. The Bible calls for tithing; it has been proven over the years that people who tithe do very well. You can't out-give the Universe or out-give God. The more you give, the more you receive.

You must also read about the wealthy, and you must learn how they accumulated their wealth. Whether it be Ray Crock, Henry Ford, John D. Rockefeller, or Lee Iococca, every successful person has a formula and a principle. Your life should never be controlled by money. My father would often say, *"I have never seen an armored car following a hearse to the cemetery."* However, I have seen people set up foundations and have wings built on hospitals where their name is etched in stone for their children, their grandchildren, and their great-grandchildren. There is life after debt.

There are many courses on money management. But money management does not have to be complex; it just has to become a habit. Spend "5 minutes" a day working on your budget, developing a plan of accumulation and debt reduction.

Remember these three formulas:

1. Don't spend more than you earn.

2. Stop using the word *"spend."* We *"give,"* we *"utilize,"* and we *"invest"* money.

3. When you use or give money, remember that it will return.

You can always say three things to your money:

1. Have a nice trip.

2. Hurry back.

3. Bring your friends.

We must first think wealth and then we must work toward it. By working toward wealth, we will obtain it, and therefore achieve our goals. Money management is a habit. Wealthy people have wealthy habits. To develop it takes only "5 minutes" a day.

Actions are the seed of fate deeds grow into destiny.

Harry S. Truman

Chapter 22

Destiny or Destined—Your Choice

A man and a boy were leading their donkey down a path. On the way to town, they came to a stretch of the path that was strewn with sharp rocks that penetrated their sandals and caused their feet to blister and bleed. Several bystanders stood by, laughing at the man and the boy as they gingerly made their way along the rocky road. Finally, one bystander yelled out, *"Hey, mister, why don't you ride the donkey?"* The man stopped, thought, and responded, *"Of course, of course,"* and he mounted the animal. As he rode, his son limped along beside him. Another passerby yelled out, *"Hey, old man, why are you riding while your son is walking?"* Startled, the man responded, *"You're right, you're right."* He dismounted and hoisted his boy onto the donkey's back. After a while, another onlooker shouted, *"Hey, old man, you have a strong and healthy donkey, why don't you both ride?"* *"Of course, of course,"* the old man replied, and he and his son sat upon their donkey as it trudged down the sharp, rocky path. Eventually, they came upon a treacherous river. Its force and currents had been strengthened by recent rains, and a wooden bridge, which joined the two shores, was in disrepair. Safe passage seemed doubtful. Nevertheless, the man, his boy, and their donkey proceeded across the bridge. Beneath the bridge, they could hear the raging waters. Just as they reached the center of the river, the bridge collapsed. The man, the boy, and the donkey fell into the vicious current. Because the man and the boy were rested from their ride, they were able to muster enough strength to swim to safety, but the donkey, tired from his difficult journey, could not. It was swept to a horrible death at the hands of the mighty river.

The moral of the story is, he who follows everyone's advice may one day lose his ass.

Within your conscious, subconscious, and superconscious mind you may retain (or at least have the ability to obtain) all the intelligence that ever existed or will exist. With such knowledge, however, comes responsibility. The acceptance of personal and professional responsibility is not optional; it's mandatory. The elimination of negative thoughts and emotions is not optional; it's also mandatory. It's vital to your health, happiness, and personal effectiveness, not to mention the development of a positive mental attitude, to exercise and increase your knowledge. After all, a positive attitude is a person's passport to tomorrow. To reach your highest personal levels you must release the weight of negativity that anchors your soul and prevents you from climbing to your highest level. Like rising in a hot air balloon, you must remove weighty emotions such as fear, anxiety, and negativity, for they will hold you down. Upon release of the baggage, your life will slowly rise.

Always remember, though, that in soaring toward your dreams, potential is the first step. Direction and discipline are the second step. To reach this level you must first determine what is holding you down. Begin the process by clearing your mind. Review your entire life—past and present—in detail. Analyze each memory, thought, or situation that has had a negative effect on you. As you make your analysis, understand that you have the ability to neutralize, but also remember that what is done is done. The past is history. You cannot make the sand in an hour glass go back up. Everything we are is a culmination of our past.

The third step is to like yourself. You must like yourself and believe in yourself. When you accomplish this task, you will recognize that the negatives of the past helped build your character and have ultimately had a positive influence on your development.

In the story of the man, the boy, and the donkey, it was not the fault of the onlookers that our Biblical friend "lost his ass." When he got to the bridge, he could have used his own judgment, intelligence, and wisdom. Instead of being intent on following other people's advice and ideas, he should have evaluated the situation himself. If he had thought carefully about his predicament, he could have dispersed weight evenly upon the bridge, instead of concentrating all the weight on top of the poor donkey. It's good to listen to and accept advice, but it's simply counsel, not law. You must always review the suggestions of those around you. But ultimately the onus is on you to make an informed decision.

Abraham Lincoln said, *"Most folks are as happy as they make up their minds to be."* You could just as easily substitute *"successful"* for *"happy."* If you don't feel successful, maybe it's because you don't know what success is. Many of us were given this from our parents, teachers/rabbis, ministers/priests, or—worst of all—from television.

Many of us, most of us, confuse success with wealth.

In 1923, some of the most "successful" financiers in the country met at the Edgewater Beach Hotel in Chicago. The eminent guests included:

Charles Schwab–*President of the largest steel company in America*
Samuel Insull–*President of the largest utility company in America*
Howard Hopson–*President of the largest gas company in America*
Arthur Cutten–*the great wheat speculator*
Richard Whitney–*President of the New York Stock Exchange*
Albert Fall–*Secretary of the interior in President Harding's cabinet*
Jessie Livermore–*the greatest "bear" on wall street*
Ivar Kruegar–*Head of the world's greatest monopoly*
Leon Fraser–*President of the Bank for International Settlements*

If money could buy happiness, these men would have been in a constant state of ecstasy. But this is where they were 25 years after their famous meeting:

Charles Schwab–*went bankrupt and lived the last five years of his life on borrowed money.*

Samuel Insull–*died in a foreign land, a penniless fugitive from justice.*

Howard Hopson–*went insane.*

Arthur Cutten–*died insolvent in another country.*

Richard Whitney–*had just been released from Sing Sing prison.*

Albert Fall–*having been pardoned from prison, died at home, broke.*

Jessie Livermore–*committed suicide.*

Ivar Kruegar–*committed suicide.*

Leon Fraser–*committed suicide.*

Still think you would want to trade places with any of these men? In society's terms, they had it all, obviously they lived unsuccessfully.

People have their own ideas about what will make them happy. You may listen to their opinions, but the ultimate decision must be yours.

You and I are essentially infinite choice-makers. In every moment of our existence, we are in that field of all possibilities where we have access to an infinity of choices.

Deepak Chopra

Chapter 23

Release Your Brake

Imagine you have just purchased a brand new Rolls Royce. Now imagine that this high quality, high performance automobile has been engineered and mechanically perfected in every detail, except for one tiny mistake. A mistake was made in assembling the braking system and one of the front wheels is locked.

Let us presume that you want to take your new automobile for a drive to impress your neighbors. You get in and bask in the smell of the new leather; you start the engine, which roars to life in a quiet, yet powerful whisper; you slide the transmission into drive and ease down on the gas. Everything in this $100,000 car is perfect except for one front wheel brake. What happens when you step on the gas? The answer is simple—you spin around the locked wheel. The car goes around and around. No matter how hard you turn the wheel, no matter how hard you step on the gas, you simply go in a circle.

When you realize and accept responsibility, you release the brakes that you put on your life. The world is full of people that are just like that new Rolls Royce. They may have all the tools, but their lives continually go in circles. This is because they are holding on to one key thought or experience. Something—sometime, somehow, somewhere—put a brake on their subconscious. This is not difficult to believe, considering the tenets upon which so many of us are raised:

1. No, you can't.

2. Don't try to be somebody you aren't.

3. You're too big for your britches.

4. Don't speak unless spoken to.

5. Don't bite off more than you can chew.

6. Save for a rainy day.

7. A woman's place is in the home.

8. The Lord giveth and the Lord taketh away.

9. I'll believe it when I see it.

10. Men are from Mars, women are from Venus.

My wife and I learned a hard lesson, but we also came to learn more about life. In my latest book, *Dying to Be Young*, I shared the *lessons of life* from my father.

"5 Minute" Lessons of Life

1. Life is about choices—choose wisely.

2. We are put on Earth to grow, to evolve.

3. Only humans have free will—will to be free.

4. You must know the difference between right and wrong.

5. Follow the path of your heart and you've made the right decision.

6. There is no right way to do the wrong thing.

7. Manifest your life as you choose and the universe will assist you.

8. Death is simply a passing from one dimension of life to another.

9. Those who seek truth are seeking to be one with God; God is truth.

10. The future of your life is in your vision today—see clearly.

On the best sunny day, the most powerful magnifying glass will not light paper if you keep moving the glass. But if you focus and hold it, the paper will light up. That is the power of concentration.

> Ralph Waldo Emerson, the famous poet and essayist, was out one day trying to get a calf into the barn. But he made the common mistake of thinking only of what he wanted. Emerson pushed and his son pulled, but the calf stiffened his legs and stubbornly refused to leave the pasture.
>
> The Irish housemaid saw their predicament. She couldn't write essays and books, but on this occasion at least, she had more horse sense, or calf sense, than Emerson. She put her maternal finger in the calf's mouth and let the calf suck her finger as she gently led him into the barn.
>
> The lesson is simple but profound:
>
> The best way to influence others is by considering their desires, not just your own.
>
> From *How to Win Friends and Influence People* by Dale Carnegie

It only takes "5 minutes" a day to think about success. Spend "5 minutes" now concentrating on you and what you need to do to become more successful.

My thoughts for success are as follows:

"5 Minute" Thoughts for Success

- You can never change your outer world without first changing your inner thoughts.

- Don't *wish* for things to get better in your life; *actively* work to make things better in your life.

- Be solution conscious. Focus 10% on the problem and 90% on the solution.

- The future is your tree—plant it today. The choices you make today will shape your tomorrow.

- Build a reputation on delivering more than you promised. It comes back to you like a tidal wave.

No one can stop you from reaching your goals unless you give them permission to do so. Don't give permission.

Find out what is holding you back, locate the cause, and address it. Only then will your symptoms dissipate. Be your own person. Do not allow your life to become a quagmire. You are where you are because you put yourself there. Take responsibility and make any changes that are necessary. Thomas Edison said, *"There is a better way for everything—find it."*

There are two primary choices in life; to accept conditions as they exist, or accept the responsibility for changing them.

Dennis Waitley

Chapter 24

The Choice is Yours

Norman Vincent Peale said, *"Empty pockets never held anyone back; only empty heads and empty hearts can do that."* We must begin by loving life, and loving life begins by loving ourselves. Mahatmas Gandhi said, *"Where there is love there is life."* Our love of life is ingrained within us. Often, to make a difference in life, we must make a difference in ourselves, and many times this difference is a culmination of choices. We are what we are today because of the choices we made yesterday and we will be what we are tomorrow because of the choices that we make today. We must live, prosper, and die by our choices. Some choices are easier than others. We must decide what time to get out of bed, what to wear, what to eat, when to exercise, where to work, where to go to school, whom to marry, and how to discipline our children.

Choices are ours and we can only make them based on whatever experience we have acquired over the years or the experience that we have learned from others. If we don't like our situation, we can change our attitudes, change our choices, and change our lives. Sometimes it's difficult to change our attitudes. Sometimes it's more difficult to choose. But if we must, we can, because we can do whatever we want. We must choose what we feel is best for us, for our family, for humanity. Our choices must be based upon giving. Our choices must be based upon logic.

In my lectures, I tell the story of a wealthy oil baron in Texas who decided it was time for his young daughter to marry. He invited a large group of the most recognized young gentlemen from Dallas to his home. They all stood at one end of the swimming pool, which was filled with alligators, while his daughter stood at the other end. The Texas gentleman looked at this group of eligible bachelors and said, *"Any man who can jump into the pool and swim to the other end can have the following three things: They can have a large ranch and a home; they can have five million dollars; and they can have my daughter's hand in marriage."*

No sooner did the oil baron finish talking when there was a large splash into the pool. The man responsible for that splash swam with fervor from one end to the other. When the suitor jumped out of the water, the wealthy gentleman jumped up and shook his hand, gushing, *"Congratulations, son, you made it, you made it!"* He continued, *"What do you want first—the money, the ranch, or my daughter?"*

"None," the young man replied.

The puzzled baron asked, *"Well, what do you want?"*

The young man answered, *"I want the name of the man who pushed me into the pool!"*

Many times in life, we enter situations because we are pushed into them. We might not choose it, but we choose to survive within that situation. Our innate desire to succeed is a master motivator. In life, there are two approaches: the right approach and the wrong approach. With both come consequences. But the consequences will be based upon your decision, which was in turn based upon your approach. When you reach a crossroads or fork in the road of your life, you must choose. You must choose according to your beliefs, choose according to what has happened in your past and by utilizing the resources of your past experience. You must choose based upon your predictions of the future. Choices aren't always cut and dry, right or wrong, they are simply choices. We need to do whatever we must do for the good of everyone involved. You are and always will be a product of your choices. Choices are difficult, but there is a definite line between right and wrong.

When one makes the right choice, he never has to worry about the outcome. It's like telling the truth. My father used to say,
 When you lie, you have to cover it up with another lie, another story, and another fabrication. Choices are up to the individual. Make the right choice. Exercise this skill for "5 minutes" each and every day when you're confronted with choices.

Ask yourself, *Did I make the easy choice or did I make the right choice?*

Remind yourself that the choices you make today will determine where you will be tomorrow.

Thinking positively is always a choice and there is no scientific how-to guidebook for positive thinking. You can only be provided with the basics, every step beyond that is completely up to you, it's a choice. We all have options each and every day for how we deal with events that arise that would potentially fill our thoughts with negativity. We are the only ones that can make the choice of whether or not we'll allow this to happen. For some of us, this will be the most difficult component of thinking positively: making the choice and accepting the responsibility for our thoughts. We like to think that we can't control our thoughts and while there are times when our thoughts invade our conscious minds, for the most part, we can control them. Over time and with a great amount of practice we can learn to control our thoughts to the degree that it isn't even a conscious act, this is our choice. This chapter is about choices, take "5 minutes" each day to make the choice to be happy, to be successful, to be a better person, the choice is yours.

Mrs. Jones' dishwasher quit working, so she called a repairman. He couldn't accommodate her with an evening appointment, and since she had to go to work the next day, she told him, "*I'll leave the key under the mat. Fix the dishwasher, leave the bill on the counter, and I'll mail you the check. By the way, don't worry about my Rottweiler. He won't bother you. But, whatever you do, do not under any circumstances talk to my parrot!*"

When the repairman arrived at Mrs. Broomfield's apartment the next day, he discovered the biggest and meanest looking Rottweiler he had ever seen. But, like she had said, the dog just lay there on the carpet watching the repairman go about his business.

However, the whole time he was there, the parrot drove him nuts with his incessant squawking and talking. Finally the repairman couldn't contain himself any longer and yelled, "*Shut up, you stupid bird!*"

To which the parrot replied, "*Get him, Brutus!*"

Lesson: In life we make our own choices. We can learn by our experience or listen to the experience of others. Instructions are usually provided for a reason; you may save yourself tons of grief and pain if you follow them.

The truly amazing thing about the power of positive thinking is that it's our choice. Once we've trained our mind to do it, and formed the habit, it's a completely subconscious act. This means that while in the beginning it may be difficult to train your mind to see things and react in a positive manner, the payoff is a much better view of the world at large. I think it's worth investing "5 minutes" a day. Look at what Jim Rohn says about choice.

Any day we wish, we can discipline ourselves to change it all. Any day we wish, we can open the book that will open our mind to new knowledge. Any day we wish, we can start a new activity. Any day we wish, we can start the process of life change. We can do it immediately, or next week, or next month, or next year.

We can also do nothing. We can pretend rather than perform. And if the idea of having to change ourselves makes us uncomfortable, we can remain as we are. We can choose rest over labor, entertainment over education, delusion over truth, and doubt over confidence. The choices are ours to make. But while we curse the effect, we continue to nourish the cause. As Shakespeare uniquely observed, "The fault is not in the stars, but in ourselves." We created our circumstances by our past choices. We have both the ability and the responsibility to make better choices beginning today. Those who are in search of the good life do not need more answers or more time to think things over to reach better conclusions. They need the truth. They need the whole truth. And they need nothing but the truth.

We cannot allow our errors in judgment, repeated every day, to lead us down the wrong path. We must keep coming back to those basics that make the biggest difference in how our life works out. And then we must make the very choices that will bring life, happiness and joy into our daily lives.

And if I may be so bold to offer my last piece of advice for someone seeking and needing to make changes in their life - If you don't like how things are, change it! You're not a tree. You have the ability to totally transform every area in your life—and it all begins with your very own power of choice."

Time is life and life is time—choose to live to the fullest of your time, you do this by making smart choices. Today and each day forward take "5 minutes" each day to review your choices. If you made a choice you are not happy with—change it. The great thing about tomorrow is we don't have to make the same mistakes we made today —YOUR CHOICE!

You see things; and you say, 'Why?' But I dream things that never were; and I say, 'Why not?'

George Bernard Shaw

Chapter 25

What If

What if you were king and ruled over a magic kingdom? You could be anybody or anything. You could have anything and live any way you wish. You could create your own "fantasy island." What if?

Once a reporter approached George Bernard Shaw and asked him to play the "what if" game. The reporter asked Mr. Shaw, *"You have known royalty, top politicians, and world-renowned authors, artists, lecturers, scientists, and teachers. If you could live your life over and be any of these people or have anything they have or be any person in history, who would you want to be?"*

Shaw replied, *"I would choose to be the man George Bernard Shaw could have been, but never was."*

You see, Shaw was a realist. He realized that he could have accomplished more in his life, but he knew that he could never be anyone but himself. The magic kingdom of "what if" is bound by the limitations of self-worth and self-effort. God, in his infinite wisdom, created you to be unique and distinct. No two people contain the same cellular makeup. You are priceless, one-of-a-kind. You are like the *Mona Lisa*, never to be duplicated. You have unique talents and abilities. You will be confronted by unique opportunities, and you alone control your inner magic kingdom.

Walt Disney dreamed of being an artist. Despite continuous rejection and near bankruptcy, he continued to refine his talents and pursue his dream. When he was finally hired by a newspaper to produce artwork, he was so poor that he had to tell the editor that his shoes were in the shop and that he needed to get an advance of two dollars to get them out. However, as his success grew, so did his dreams, and with them, his self-esteem, and he grew past that embarrassment.

One day, years later, Disney called his good friend, Art Linkletter, and asked him to visit a site in southern California. While walking through the brush, Disney told Linkletter of his dream: a magic kingdom. He pointed to the future sites of Frontierland and Fantasyland. He continued to map out the entire theme park to his friend. Then he showed Linkletter where he planned to build hotels to house the millions of people who would visit his kingdom.

Art Linkletter tells this story with a smile and recalls the walk back to the car. He states that by declining Disney's proposition to invest in his dream, that walk back to the car cost him one million dollars a step. However, one shouldn't shed any tears for Art Linkletter. He came away from his meeting with Disney owning all the rights to photographs and likenesses of what is today known as Disneyland. Art Linkletter did not buy 100% into his best friend's dream. But even by buying into it by 1%, he profited. What if he hadn't had the time to meet with Disney that day? What if he hadn't had the time to be Disney's friend? What if he hadn't believed in Walt Disney?

Another man who played the "what if?" game was John Goddard. As a 15 year old boy, he made a list of 127 things he wanted to achieve in his life, including climbing Mt. Everest, exploring the Nile, running a 5-minute mile, reading the Bible cover to cover, reading the entire Encyclopedia Britannica, writing a book, playing "Claire De Lune" on the piano, riding in a submarine, and circumnavigating the globe. Today he is one of the most famous explorers in the world. He has reached 105 of his 127 goals and is still going! He plans on visiting all 141 countries in the world. Currently, to my knowledge, he has visited 111 on his journey, exploring the Amazon, Nile, and Congo rivers, and living to see the 21st century. He never wished to see things through another's eyes; he has lived his life through his own dreams and visions.

What if he wanted to be someone or somewhere else? You are unique, and because of your uniqueness no one can do exactly what you can do. No one knows exactly what you know. No one has a personality exactly like you. No one sees you as you see yourself.

The Nevada Game Commission said that George Foreman was too old to box. He had to sue for the right to fight. He had his day in court, and that was the first of the two greatest victories of his life. "What if" he had believed he was too old? "What if" he didn't go to court? "What if" he didn't dream? "What if" he didn't believe in himself?

In the inimitable words of George Foreman himself, as taken from Walt Disney, "*When you wish upon a star, makes no difference who you are. Anything your heart desires can come true.*" Plato once said that self-conquest is the greatest of all victories. The winners in this world are distinct individuals who continually use their superconscious and their innate desire to succeed regardless of what obstacles may confront them.

"*The road to success is always under construction.*" Great men have always been dreamers. Thomas Edison was a dreamer, Christopher Columbus was a dreamer, and John F. Kennedy was a dreamer. Fairy tales can come true; they can happen to you if you're young at heart.

T. E. Lawrence said, "*All men dream, but not equally. Those who dream by night in the dusty recesses of their minds wake in the day to find that it was vanity, but the dreamers of the day are dangerous men, for they may act their dreams with open eyes, to make it possible.*"

Commit "5 minutes" every day to daydream. When you see the invisible you can do the impossible.

"*Every great dream begins with a dreamer. Always remember, you have within you the strength, the patience, and the passion to reach for the stars to change the world,*" said Harriet Tubman.

These are such powerful thoughts, such powerful words that they should give strength and inspire us all. Just knowing that you have everything you need to change the world already inside of you is empowering. Being a dreamer is just the beginning to living out your greatest dreams.

If it hadn't been for great dreams, Vivaldi never would have composed "The Four Seasons," Bach "St. Matthew Passion," or Handel "Messiah." Neither would Michelangelo have created his breathtaking work in the Sistine Chapel. Leonardo da Vinci never would have sketched the first parachute and helicopter, painted such masterpieces such as *The Last Supper* and *Mona Lisa* or produced some of the first detailed illustrations of physiology of the human body.

Every single great accomplishment we have seen in this world started out with a person's vision, a great dream that then led to a particular achievement. It was the individual's courage to cultivate their dream, to not be affected by the thoughts of others that made the difference.

There have been times in your life when you were told you couldn't do something or something you were striving for was impossible to accomplish. The key is to listen to your heart and not the words of the little minds out there. As the quote above by Harriet Tubman states, you already have everything you need right inside. You also have the potential to change the world in some way, as each of these examples state.

So what are your great dreams? What great potential do you have inside of you that is just waiting to be born? Is it to write a great life-changing book? To lose weight? How about own your own business? You have the potential to create a masterpiece like Michelangelo. Maybe you want to compose another great classical piece like Vivaldi, Bach, or Handel. Or maybe you want to become a great inventor like Leonardo da Vinci?

There are no second chances in life; there is only here and now. Each day we are blessed with 86,400 seconds—invest them wisely. The sand in an hour glass doesn't go up. What if today was your last day? What if you could change your life? The good news is you can make any change right here and now. Make the choice. Make the change before it's too late.

Live Life Over

by Erma Bombeck

If I had my life to live over...

I would have talked less and listened more.

I would have invited friends over to dinner even if the carpet was stained and the sofa faded.

I would have eaten the popcorn in the 'good' living room and worried much less about the dirt when someone wanted to light a fire in the fireplace.

I would have taken the time to listen to my grandfather ramble about his youth.

I would never have insisted the car windows be rolled up on a summer day because my hair had just been teased and sprayed.

I would have burned the pink candle sculpted like a rose before it melted in storage.

I would have sat on the lawn with my children and not worried about grass stains.

I would have cried and laughed less while watching television—and more while watching life.

I would have shared more of the responsibility carried by my spouse.

I would have gone to bed when I was sick instead of pretending the earth would go into a holding pattern if I weren't there for the day.

I would never have bought anything just because it was practical, wouldn't show soil, or was guaranteed to last a lifetime.

Instead of wishing away nine months of pregnancy, I'd have cherished every moment and realized that the wonderment growing inside me was the only chance in life to assist God in a miracle.

When my kids kissed me impetuously, I would never have said, "Later. Now go get washed up for dinner."

There would have been more "I love yous," more "I'm sorrys," but mostly, given another shot at life, I would seize every minute—look at it and really see it—live it—and never give it back.

In memory of Erma Bombeck who lost her fight with cancer.

Be courageous and bold. When you look back on your life, you'll regret the things you didn't do more than the ones you did."

Maybe your dream is just to make a positive difference in this world in your own special way. Whatever it may be, I challenge you to spend "5 minutes" per day to dream a great dream and then go out into this world and live it. You may be surprised at what you are capable of accomplishing; you may be the next great thing to go down in history.

Spend "5 minutes" a day dreaming. Close your eyes and see your life as you want it to be.

What if you had the ability to change your life? What if you had the ability to achieve your dreams? What if you had the ability to obtain the unobtainable? What if you had the ability to turn the ordinary into something extraordinary?

What if you spent "5 minutes" a day dreaming, planning, and coordinating your destiny? You can change your life in "5 minutes" a day. No more ifs, ands, or buts—just do's.

Put yourself in a comfortable position, close your eyes, and see the world as a better place to live in. See what you can do to make it a better place to live in. See yourself as a better person. Follow the path that will take you in that direction. Dream of your wants and desires and then create a plan to make your dreams become your reality.

Try not to become a man of success, but rather try to become a man of value.

Albert Einstein

Chapter 26

The Road to Success is Always Under Construction

Anyone can get on the road to success. The secret is to remember that "the road to success is always under construction." There will always be obstacles. Success does not follow the path of least resistance; this is why man created detours. As we journey on the road to success, we are continually jockeying for position.

Rule #1: Have a finger or something point to it. Life is not so much a matter of position as it is disposition.

Rule #2: The success of your life is navigated by the quality of your thoughts. Good thoughts equal a good life; bad thoughts equal a bad life.

The great German philosopher, Goethe, set forth the following principles for a more successful and well-balanced life:

1. Health enough to make work a pleasure.

2. Wealth enough to support your needs.

3. Strength enough to battle difficulties and overcome them.

4. Patience enough to toil until some good has been accomplished.

5. Grace enough to toil until some good has been accomplished.

6. Try enough to toil until some good has been accomplished.

7. Love enough to move you to be useful and helpful to others.

8. Faith enough to make real things of God.

9. Hope enough to remove all fears concerning the future.

Goethe's creed may provide you with the basis on which to create your map of success. Your superconsciousness gives you the knowledge and the power. Man's greatest source of power is the superconscious mind. It can be influenced to work toward your desired goal in all your waking hours. It continues the journey through thought, concept, imagination, and expectation, even while you sleep.

In an interview with Napoleon Hill, Woodrow Wilson stated, *"The state of mind in which I ask help of my subconscious seems to have much to do with results. In times of great emergency, under the stress of intense emotion, the guidance and need come quickly. If there is any doubt in my mind, I also find the result is generally negative. But when my belief is so intense that I almost feel myself in possession of the answer to my problems, then the result is always positive."* Napoleon Hill then went on to state, *"Wilson was convinced that the subconscious mind is the gateway to the infinite intelligence of our creator and could be used effectively only through that mental attitude of complete belief known as faith. When you harmonize your mind with that of your creator, you can gain guidance, power, and revelation not available to you by any other means."*

My total commitment is to the wellness-based philosophy: wellness care versus crisis care. On a weekly basis, obstetricians and gynecologists write 2,645,000 prescriptions for antibiotics alone. During that same week, interns give out 1,416,000 prescriptions. Pediatricians and family physicians prescribe 500 million dollars worth of antibiotics for the treatment of one problem: ear infections in children.

The New England Journal of Medicine said that three out of four children who have taken amoxicillin for ear infections will have recurrent problems. In addition, another 500 million dollars is spent on pediatric illnesses.

The man who discovered penicillin, Alexander Fleming, warned that overuse of this bacterium might lead to problems with bacteria resistance. The foresight of Alexander Fleming was greatly ignored by the medical establishment until recently. In a recent *Time* magazine article, "Revenge of the Killer Microbes," the sub-headline ran, "New Viruses and Drug Resistant Bacteria are Reversing Human Victories over Infectious Diseases."

Newsweek published an article, "Antibiotics, The End of Miracle Drugs." This was encapsulated with a warning sign that read, "No Longer Effective against Killer Bugs."

Yet, with this literature and knowledge of the past 15 years, antibiotic prescriptions to children have risen by a staggering 51%.

Jerry Seinfeld, the king of metaphors, in his book *SeinLanguage*, said everybody wants to be healthy. The amazing thing is that nobody knows where to begin. We need to begin with the basics, and we need to begin by spending "5 minutes" a day trying to understand the role of prevention. The May 29th, 1997 headline of *USA Today* said that 30 billion dollars was spent ineffectively on cancer research and that we must change our paradigm, not just concentrating on disease, but working on its prevention. Prevention is the key to the future.

T. McCowen, in his book, *The Role of Medicine: Dream, Mirage, or Nemesis*, stated, *"After congressional studies of the issues, it has become a general consensus that 40–60% of all antibiotics in this country are misrepresented."* As we head to the next millennium, we must ask ourselves one basic question: Is the health crisis today based on inflated medical costs or just poor results? Nutrition is being influenced by the converters of trends in health care. Business, government, and many different trends are moving us from a sickness care system to one of wellness care. The medical profession is both confused and concerned. Dean Burwell, MD, while addressing medical students at Harvard University, summed it up like this, *"Half of what we have taught you is wrong. Unfortunately, we dont know which half."*

Is that to say that medicine is obsolete? No. But it does indicate that people are also searching for answers. The wellness approach is no longer a concept, but a movement. Medical doctors today are joining forces with chiropractors at a record pace, a symbiotic relationship based on the results of the wellness principle. Julian Whitaker, MD, is the author of five books, including, *Reversing Heart Disease.* He states, *"It's a crime how the medical industry treats you. It's wrong to ignore you until you get sick, especially since we know how to prevent illness. It's wrong to automatically reach for a needle, a scalpel, or a prescription pad."*

We are a world at war, not just in the Middle East, but in each of our homes. Below I share with you a passage that I first read in a book called *Wellness* written by my friend and classmate, Dr. Bob Hoffman. Dr. Bob is now CEO of the "Masters Circle," a consulting company. He is an icon in our profession. I am proud he was my classmate and even prouder to call him my friend.

Each and every one of us is at war: a germ warfare that we fight every day in our homes and our offices. The war that we face is the Healthcare War sweeping America. Just consider these facts:

Healthcare spending in our country exceeds 1.8 trillion dollars, which is 4 times the amount spent on national defense and 40 times the amount spent on homeland security. According to a recent Harvard study, 50% of all bankruptcies in our country are the direct result of excessive medical spending. This is compounded by Warren Sick's article in the *Washington Post* where he reported that every 30 seconds someone files for bankruptcy due to serious medical problems. Some experts believe that retiring couples will need between $200,000 and $300,000 just to pay for the most basic medical coverage.

If this is not enough to make you sick, in a recent article published in the *Journal of the American Medical Association*, Dr. Barbara Starfield of Johns Hopkins School of Hygiene and Public Health listed the negative health effects in the U.S. system itself, including:

- 7,000 deaths per year from medication errors in hospitals

- 12,000 deaths per year from unnecessary surgery

- 8 million unnecessary hospitalizations

- 3 million unnecessary long-term hospital admissions

- 199,000 unnecessary deaths per year

- 20,000 deaths per year from other errors in hospitals

- 77 million unnecessary prescriptions

- 77 billion in unnecessary costs

AIDS takes less than 20,000 lives per year and the publicity is enormous, yet 199,000 die from unnecessary medical care every year and this epidemic seems to be ignored.

According to Dr. David Himmelstein, associate professor at Harvard Medical School, we are all one serious illness away from bankruptcy. Another Harvard professor, Dr. Steffie Woolander said in an interview, *"Even the best policies in this country have so many loopholes; it's easy to build up thousands of dollars in expenses."*

The War on Drugs is the #1 cause of the Healthcare Crisis that exists today. My goal in life is to make a difference in the Healthcare Crisis. The adulation of drugs and surgery that dominates our country's consciousness needs to be changed. We need to stop treating the symptoms; we need to treat and remove the cause. I must do more than live to be young, I must get myself healthy enough to lead by example and strong enough to tell my message.

It's time for the consumer to be educated and to make a choice. The choice must be an educated one, and we must commit ourselves to fulfill this potential, to fulfill our calling to heal ourselves. How we choose to live our lives is a reflection of who and what we are. We must not be victims of a healthcare delivery system that is out of control. We, the consumers, must inevitably take control. Even though we are all unique, we share certain common elements. Our capacity for learning and intellect is inherent in us as rational human beings.

I have always believed that *"the power that creates the body can heal the body."* There is no cure for botulism, yet I'm alive and well. When I was first able to write, and still not able to speak, I asked my doctor, one of my best friends, Dr. Dennis Egitto to have 5,000 milligrams of vitamin C and 2,000 milligrams of B complex put into my IV solution. At first the hospital said no, but my argument was for $10,000 a day (the cost of our care, per person), this was not the most unreasonable request. The body, given the right tools, can heal itself.

- A body has the capability to repair itself continually at a rate of 2 billion cells per day.

More specifically, our body completely replaces:

- our skin about every 20 days

- our stomach about once a month

- our liver about every 6 weeks

- our skeleton about every three months

- all of our brain cells annually

What this means is—if you didn't like yourself yesterday, don't worry, you'll be a completely new person in no time at all. You are physically changing all the time. You simply need to decide to take action and change for the better.

What if I told you one company, with a team of Nobel prize-winning doctors, is looking for a way to turn back the clock? What if you could "age youthfully?" One doctor has done this by working with telomerase, an enzyme that maintains the ends of our cells' chromosomes. These ends are called telomeres. Telomeres get shorter each time a cell divides, and when they get too short, the cell can no longer make fresh copies of itself. If we live long enough, the tissues and organ systems that depend on continued cell replication begin to falter. The skin sags, the internal organs grow slack, the immune system response weakens such that the next chest cold could be our last.

Dr. Andrews of Isagenix states, *"Make poor lifestyle choices, and you're likely to die of heart disease or cancer or something well before your telomeres would otherwise become life-threateningly short."* Dr. Andrews believes that anyone who takes reasonable care of himself and takes supplements loaded with antioxidants may activate telomerase and thus slow down the baseline rate at which the body falls apart. Dr. Andrews likens the underlying causes of aging to sticks of dynamite, with truncated telomeres being the stick with the shortest fuse. Telomeres also assist cell division. Every time a cell splits, the ends of its chromosomes fail to get fully copied in the two new daughter cells, and a bit of telomeric DNA gets lost. No harm is done to the rest of the chromosome, but in cells that divide frequently, the telomeres shorten with each replication. Telomerase's job is to synthesize new DNA to add to the shrinking telomeres, slowing down the decline.

What if you could turn back the clock—would you do it? What if you could do it healthily and naturally with no side effects. Over the past few years, the case for telomeres as a major player in aging, possibly even the prime mover, has grown stronger. *"Heart health,"* a telomere biologists point out, *"depends heavily on the endothelial cells that line the blood vessels and brain health on the Schwann cells that make the myelin that protects neurons, all of which are cell types that hear the ticking of the mitotic clock."*

According to a recent article last year, Harvard University researcher

Ron DePinho published two studies in the journal *Nature* that have reframed the debate about telomerase activation. DePinho created an ingenious model whereby he could turn telomerase off in a mouse and then restore it, simply by administering or withholding a synthetic estrogen drug. In the first study, the mice with turned-off telomerase exhibited signs and symptoms of decrepitude akin to what we might endure at the age of 80 or 90: wrinkled skin, sluggish intestines, and a shrunken brain. When telomerase production was turned back on, the tissues rejuvenated within a month.

There is a substitute to drugs and surgery, only a philosophical difference may stand in your way to look and fell younger. Do your own homework research and don't let others' philosophies impact yours. To learn more about telomeres and *youthful aging*, go to www.5minutemotivator.com.

There is a philosophical concept called tabula rasa, which means blank slate. The theory behind tabula rasa is that we are all born with the same intellectual capacity. Our own intellect, which is a major part of who we are, is nurtured by forces to which we are exposed. In the past, forces such as family, religion, and books were the prevailing influences on our intellectual development. Unfortunately, these forces have been replaced by other, less cerebral influences. Television is an example of just such an influence. TV has been a major contributor to our educational decline. Although it gives us access to many educational stations, it's estimated that less than 5% of our population views these. The average household watches in excess of four hours of TV a day, and children spend more time in front of the TV than they spend with their parents. Who is raising our children? Who creates their vision? What TV program is molding their dreams? What TV commercials are setting their health paradigm?

Whether or not you accept the concept of tabula rasa, there is strong evidence to support it. There seems to be little to indicate that the average person's intellect has improved over the ages. The earliest known alphabet was far more complex than the one we use today. Astronomers declared the earth was round before the birth of Christ, and even measured it to within a few feet of the size modern scientists claim the earth to be. Regardless of what you believe in terms of intellectual capacity, it's important to realize that scientists still do not fully understand the human mind. The easiest way to look at it, however, is as one looks at the computer. A computer basically does three things:

> *Processes information*
> *Calculates information*
> *Stores information*

However, before a computer can perform these tasks, it must be given a list of directions called a program. Once programmed, it can perform its designated tasks in milliseconds. It computes, tabulates, records, recommends, organizes, and corrects over and over again without hesitation or complaint. It never asks for a raise, except possibly megabytes of memory, nor does it demand vacation, sick leave, or maternity leave.

Our intellect is comprised of conscious, subconscious, and superconscious functions in a program response system. This response is based on our programming, our mindset, on all facets, responses, and reactions in our life. The old adage, garbage in, garbage out, holds little context here. But what if we programmed our computer with healthy habits based upon sound levels of nutrition and diet? It would only take us "5 minutes" a day to re-program our computer. Once we perceive how we respond to the directions contained in our programs, we realize our intelligence is computer-like. However, there are three major differences between upbringing and your basic computer:

> *We control and program our own computer.*
> *No one else, without our permission, can alter our program.*
> *We have unlimited capacity, for we and we alone turn our computers on and off.*

The exciting message in this metaphor is that we can program ourselves for whatever we choose and for whomever we choose it. Not all people have lived under the best of conditions, yet they've maintained health. Dr. Victor E. Frankel, author of *Man's Search for Meaning*, stated, *"We who lived in concentration camps can remember the men who walked through the huts comforting others, giving away their last piece of bread. They may have been few in number, but they offer sufficient proof that everything can be taken from a man, save for one thing: the last of his freedoms to choose one's attitude in any given set of circumstances; to choose one's own way."*

Spend the next "5 minutes" choosing your way. Choose the direction of your health; choose the direction of your happiness. Create a model, and program that model. As Winston Churchill once said, *"Never, never, never give up."* The road to success may always be under construction, but it's a road that we define, we alter, we build for ourselves.

If at first you don't succeed, you're running about average.
M.H. Alderson

Chapter 27

If You Want a Place in the Sun,
Prepare to Put Up with a Few Blisters

Some of the greatest success stories in history resulted from words or acts of encouragement from others. Had it not been for a woman named Sophia, we might never have been blessed with the works of one literary genius.

One cold, snowy, winter day, Nathaniel went home a heartbroken man. He gathered up his courage to tell Sophia, his wife, that he was fired from his job. Instead of sharing his moan of dejection, she surprised her husband with an exclamation of joy. *"Now you can write your book,"* she responded.

"Sure," replied Nathaniel. *"And what will we live on while I am writing it?"*

To his surprise, she opened a drawer and pulled out a box filled with money.

"Where on earth did you get so much money?" asked Nathaniel.

"From the day I first met you, I knew that there was a genius within you, and you were destined for greatness. So, each week I put aside some of the money that you gave me. I knew that one day you would write a great book," replied Sophia.

From her faith, confidence, and belief came one of the greatest novels of American literature, *The Scarlet Letter* by Nathaniel Hawthorne.

W. Clement Stone said, *"There is little difference in people, but that little difference makes a big difference."* The little difference is attitude and the big difference is whether it's positive or negative. Attitude gave a quiet, unassuming man, who was a lawyer by trade and a pacifist by principle, the power to topple a vast empire. Mahatma Gandhi changed the future of India and made an impossible vision possible. He stated, *"When I believe I cannot do something, I am unable to do it. But when I believe I can, I acquire the ability even if I didn't have the ability in the beginning."* One of the secrets of success is to make a public commitment, one so forceful that you cannot turn back from it. Each of us has innate ability, power, and resource that, coupled with belief, will enable us to achieve all we have ever dreamed of.

Nike is famous for the line from their commercial, *"Bo knows... Just Do It."* Bo Jackson has not only been an athletic icon, but an inspiration to any athlete who was ever injured. Never in the history of sports has any man been able to come back from a hip replacement surgery to play a professional sport again. His later career was filled with commitment to overcome an obstacle that no man had ever done before. His attitude made the difference.

Bo Jackson made a decision to succeed regardless of what the medical community told him. Where does a man develop these qualities? As a boy, Bo didn't always know. One day a seventh-grade bully beat him up. Vowing revenge, he got hold of a gun and tracked down his tormentor. But just before he fired, he wondered, *What would happen to me if I pulled the trigger?* An image more embarrassing and life-altering than being beaten up came to focus. Bo visualized a life in jail. He changed his aim and fired at a tree instead.

Dudley Moore is best remembered for his comedy relationship with Peter Cook. This diminutive comic stood a tiny 5' 2.5" and had extensive treatment for a club foot as a child. His start in life was bleak, but he was a notorious giggler and was easily provoked into fits of giggles by Cook during their live shows. Moore was an excellent musician and had left his working class roots to attend Magdalen College at Oxford on a musical scholarship. Sadly, he succumbed to progressive supranuclear palsy in 2002. His last words were, *"I can hear the music all around me."*

Mia Hamm is a legendary sportswoman who, in her career as a professional soccer player, scored more goals internationally than any other soccer player, male or female, in the history of soccer. She is an inspiration to sports men and women everywhere, not least of all for her courage and conviction. Born with a club foot, she spent years in casts to repair the foot and allow her to dominate women's soccer and to be chosen as one of FIFA's best players by Pelé.

Damon Wayans is one of ten children from a highly creative family of comedians, actors, directors, and producers. He was born with a club foot that he used for two of his comedy roles. He is irreverent and witty and never allowed his difficult start to interfere with his wry humorous take on life.

Growing up a Yankees fan, one of the greatest feats I've ever seen was from a pitcher born with one hand, Jim Abbott. He's now a motivational speaker and I share with you from one of his speeches.

It's Not What's Gone, But What's Given

Not too long ago, a little girl in my neighborhood was born without a hand. She was born just after my own second daughter, Ella, was born. Her parents were obviously shaken up. About a week later, I saw them at a neighborhood function and they came over to me and asked what my thoughts were, if I had any advice for them and for their daughter. My advice? This is their daughter's life and they were asking my advice? Talk about humbling. What do you say? I had nothing very smart to say.

I told myself I wouldn't let that happen again. That it was important that I could share what I have learned.

I've learned that there are millions of people out there

ignoring disabilities and accomplishing incredible feats. I learned that you can learn to do things differently, but do them just as well. I've learned that it's not the disability that defines you, it's how you deal with the challenges the disability presents you with. I've learned that we have an obligation to the abilities we do have, not the disability.

I was born without my right hand. I have never felt slighted. As a kid I was pretty coordinated and growing up I loved sports. I learned to play baseball like most kids, playing catch with my Dad in the front yard. The only difference was that we had to come up with a method to throw and catch with the same hand. What we came up with, is basically what I continued to do my whole life. I used to practice by pretending to be my favorite pitchers. I'd throw a ball against a brick wall on the side of our house, switching the glove off and on, moving closer to the wall, forcing myself to get that glove on faster and faster. I imagined myself becoming a successful athlete.

Growing up, sports were my way of gaining acceptance. I guess somewhere deep inside I was thinking if I was good enough on the field then maybe kids wouldn't think of me as being so different. Honestly I hid behind sports. I wanted the attention that comes from being successful, but I was very reluctant to draw any attention to my disability You know, it's funny, there was an article in the *LA Times* recently about a high school pitcher who has been doing very well, despite missing one hand. He mentioned my name as an example, but went on to say he didn't want to be like me, he wanted to be like Randy Johnson. At first my feelings were hurt, but then I understood. That's exactly the same way I felt growing up. I didn't want to be defined by a disability. Focus on my pitching and not my hand.

I loved throwing a baseball. It's so important to find something in life you feel crazy about. Because you are so passionate you naturally practice, the hard work that it takes to do something well will come easily.

You know how it worked out. I got to play baseball at the University of Michigan, 2 United States teams, The 1987 Pan American team, and the 1988 United States Olympic team. Even though I played in the major leagues for almost 10 years, the Olympics are still one of my favorite memories.

You know in my career I once won 18 games in a year. I also lost 18 games in one year. I was fortunate enough to go straight from the Olympic team to the major leagues, never spending a day in the minors. I was also sent down to the minor leagues after 8 years in the big leagues. In 1996, I went 2–18 with a 7-run error. I couldn't get anyone out. I was in the first year of a long-term contract with a team near my home. It was supposed to be easy. That following year I was fired and I drove back to California, crying all the way. I spent that summer up in Michigan hurting and wondering if my career was over. Somewhere deep inside I wasn't sure. So I called the Chicago White Sox for a try out.

They gave me a chance to pitch again. I would watch the major leagues on TV with the rest of those kids and it felt like a million miles away. That had been my life. I was away from my family who I knew thought I was crazy. Then I got the call I was going to Chicago, back to the show. That was the good news; the bad news was facing the Yankees Saturday night. They were about 100 and 15 at the time. I went on to win that game against the Yankees. In fact I went 5–0 the rest of that September.

I would like to tell those parents back in my neighborhood how wonderful my own parents were and are. They encouraged me to participate, but didn't dwell on every move I made. I don't ever remember a concession to the fact that I had one hand. Maybe even a little more was expected. I will always be thankful that they never allowed my hand to be used as an excuse.

I would like to tell that little girl, "Go out and find what it is that you love. It may not be the most obvious choice or the most logical, but never let that stop you." Baseball was hardly the most the most logical choice for someone with one hand, but I loved it, so that's what I pursued. No matter where the road takes you, don't give up until you know in your heart you done everything you possibly could to make your dreams come true. You owe nothing to disability, ignore it. When you fail, get back up and try again. Leave no room for an excuse. Don't listen to what you can't do. 99% of the time I never think of missing a hand. I've never been envious of someone with two hands. Listen to that voice deep within you, it knows when you've done your best.

Somehow, when things are said and done, there'll be some accountability. Imagine someone coming up to you at the end of your life and saying, "You've been given these talents, what did you do with them?" There is a certain potential we owe it to ourselves to live up to. Work hard, don't look back, celebrate the blessings in your life."

Jim Abbott, famed one-handed major league baseball player

Every moment, every act or action, can alter our destiny. In the movie *Mr. Destiny*, James Belushi was an executive caught in the whirlpool of depression based upon one incident in his past: he struck out while at bat in the Big Game. Throughout his whole life he hosted the anguish of that personal defeat. Michael Caine played the bartender who, through a magical elixir, led Belushi to relive his past to hit the home run, thus altering his destiny. This modern remake of the Christmas epic, *It's A Wonderful Life*, demonstrates the magic of every moment. Everything happens for a reason. Universal Law: Every action has an equal or opposite reaction. Both James Stewart and Jim Belushi's characters learned their lessons through spiritual experiences.

Wherever you are at this moment is where you have chosen to be. Wherever you are in the future is where you choose to be. Our days are filled with choices. Make each one count. Napoleon Hill said, *"The starting point of all achievement is desire."* Keep this constantly in mind. Weak desires bring weak results. Just a small amount of fire makes a small amount of heat. Bo knows, Bo knew, Bo desired. This boy grew to be Bo Jackson. Gandhi made decisions that made him Gandhi as we know him. Our present actions create our future circumstances. How we react to these circumstances creates our destiny. We are close, close to being the person we want to be, close to achieving our goals, realizing our dreams. Yes, if you want a place in the sun, prepare to put up with a few blisters.

Happiness is found in doing, not merely possessing.

Napoleon Hill

Chapter 28

Magic Seed

The fable of *Jack and the Beanstalk* is a classic. Many of us need to venture forth, as did Jack, selling his prized cow for magic seeds, only to be sneered at and ridiculed. This did not detour Jack from his beliefs, and he ventured forward and planted his magic seeds. The rest, as they say, is history.

My whole life l have ventured forth armed with magic seeds called affirmations. I plant and cultivate these every day, every week—seeds of hope, wisdom, and success. Often auspicious or inauspicious people hand them to us free of charge. We need to seed and cultivate our gardens; the need to work in the garden never ends. It's never finished, never done. My grandfather used to say, *"The cows never stay milked and the grass never stays mowed."* Every completion has a new beginning.

It's not what you harvest that makes you successful, it's what you do with your harvest that determines your success. Many considered Golda Maier a common woman. Yet, her inner strength, beauty, and desire led her to be the Prime Minister of Israel. Who would have believed that Margaret Thatcher lived over her father's grocery store until the age of 21? Yet, within her grew the seed of confidence to lead England through tumultuous times.

Some seeds take longer to germinate than others. Grandma Moses didn't start painting until she was in her 70s, yet she painted 500 celebrated works of art. Then there was Auguste Renoir. No one liked his work. One Parisian expert looked over his paintings and sneered, *"You are, I presume, dabbling in paint to amuse yourself."* Renoir replied, *"Of course. When it ceases to amuse me I will stop painting."*

Earle Nightingale, in his radio program, *Our Changing World*, told this story of Renoir. His story explained that everyone told Renoir to give up painting because he had no talent. A group of artists all rejected by the art establishment formed their own little support group. The group consisted of unknown artists Degas, Asorau, Monet, Cezanne, and Renoir. They were five men following their desires, planting their seeds of greatness on canvas. Known as the Impressionists, those who were then scorned are now recognized as masters.

The story does not end here. Years later, when Renoir was suffering from rheumatism, he was visited by Matisse. Matisse asked, *"Why is it that you still have to work? Why do you continue to torture yourself?"* Renoir slowly responded, *"The pain passes, but the pleasure of the creation of beauty remains."* Within each of us are these seeds of greatness. We must till the soil all our lives to harvest our success. Gail Brooke Burkett, in her book, *Special Days to Remember*, wrote the following poem:

> *I do not ask to walk smooth paths*
> *Nor bear an easy load*
> *I pray for strength and fortitude*
> *To climb the rock-strewn road.*
> *Give me such courage*
> *I can scale the hardest peaks alone,*
> *And transform every stumbling block*
> *Into a stepping stone.*

Many of us do not recognize the seeds of greatness. We must visualize in order to realize, for visualization is the first step to realization. Many of us are altered by our fears or detoured by our rejections. We must weed out those predators from our gardens. The seed of greatness in each of us is the ability to plant love within the hearts and souls of those around us. Visualization is simply seeing what you want to happen. What you see is what you get; you get what you see in your mind's eye. This is the most helpful way of receiving anything. This does work for everyone. Visualization is one of the strongest and fastest ways to activate your master motivator, one of the strongest and fastest ways to fill your needs, wants, dreams, and desires. It's the most incredible way of obtaining anything we want. Remember, visualization empowers your subconscious and superconscious. The mind cannot recognize the difference between an experience that is real or imagined. It does not know the difference between an experience that is really happening and one that you are going over and over in your mind the way you want it to happen. If you continually visualize something, your mind starts believing that that is exactly the way it's supposed to be.

Grandma said, *"he mowed a fine lawn."* Those are the words of affirmation Dennis Waitley recalls hearing as a young child. It's no wonder, then, that every Saturday, Waitley would hop on his bike and ride 20 miles each way to her house.

One of my favorite authors, Dennis Waitley has created a life based on the belief that the power of the mind can overcome almost any obstacle. He is an internationally-known speaker and consultant whose clients have included astronauts, Olympic athletes, Fortune 500 executives, and Super Bowl champions. He has spoken to youth groups, soldiers, entrepreneurs, and world leaders. His words of wisdom have been recorded in best-selling books and audio programs, such as *The Psychology of Winning*, *Seeds of Greatness*, and *Empires of the Mind* and have been translated and distributed around the world.

Waitley did not come from a privileged background. Back in 1942, Waitley felt anything but influential. Still a boy, he was suddenly the man of the house. He turned to his Superman books for guidance, feeling like he must deal with his feelings like Superman would. He had to be strong. His mother was struggling with her own outlook, and what she saw translated negatively to her three children. There was no child support, and the Waitley children often felt like their existence was an inconvenience to their mother.

To replenish his strength, Waitley visited his grandmother. She taught him to look beyond his circumstances and become the person he was meant to be. Grandma also introduced Waitley to the world of books. She was a proofreader and she and her husband owned a bookstore. Waitley acquired his first library card because of her influence.

Then his eighth-grade teacher gave him an influential gift: *As a Man Thinketh* by James Allen. The impact on Waitley was twofold. He felt affirmed by the positive words of another person, and the author of the book portrayed individuals as gardeners, planting seeds that would affect the future. Just like Grandma.

Waitley tells of one particularly poignant memory. *"We planted a garden together. I was amazed that the tiny seeds we were burying in the ground would become something we would later harvest and eat."* In response to his wonder, Grandma told Waitley that they were planting seeds of greatness. Years later, her answer became the title of his New York Times Bestseller, *Seeds of Greatness*.

This was not a man who just talked the talk, he tells the story of his own seeds and how his great and prolific career started. *"I approached a white-jacketed scientist busy working on formulas and asked him what he was doing,"* Waitley says. *"He engaged in conversation with me and asked me what I did for a living."* Before the discourse ended, the scientist, Dr. Jonas Salk, inventor of the polio vaccine, offered Waitley the job of being the fundraiser for the Salk Institute. *"Dr. Salk was an introvert and despised the task of talking to groups of people to raise funds for the Institute,"* Waitley says. *"He saw that I loved to speak and felt I was a great fit."* The only concern Salk had was Waitley's lack of scientific understanding. He encouraged Waitley to acquire a postgraduate degree in psychology. So he did.

Salk was not able to offer Waitley an increase in salary, but he compensated him in a way that would pay huge dividends: introducing

Waitley to his peers. "*Because he was such a well-known scientist, he was able to introduce me to people I never would have met otherwise,*" Waitley says.

"*During this time, I learned that if you're not doing what your passion is, you're putting it on layaway,*" Waitley says. "*One might work at something simply to receive a paycheck, but any free time should be used in pursuit of one's ultimate goal.*"

When asked what he would say to someone trying to break free from generations of failure, Waitley recommends studying the biographies of successful people. "*Remember, most successful people don't enjoy that success until later in life,*" he says. "*It's also important to determine your gifts, focus on them, and be you. Chase your passion and not your pension, and, of course, make certain that you hang around optimists.*"

Waitley planted many seeds in his life, but he was not alone in this concept. Planting seeds is nothing more then fertilizing or working your goals. Before you can realize anything, you must visualize something.

To add impact to visualization, you must add one additional ingredient. You must plant the seed of excitement. Ralph Waldo Emerson said, "*Nothing great was ever achieved without enthusiasm.*" We must understand that through visualization, we can activate our inner eye, the eye that creates an inner world of peace, harmony, and tranquility; an eye that can transform our dreams into reality. Every person has the capability and capacity to visualize. Close your eyes and see yourself on a field surrounded by mountains and hills. Smell the clean fresh air. Feel the dirt underneath your feet. See yourself healthy and happy. Visualization creates realization. But you must not only visualize, you must feel. You must feel through every fiber, every cell of your being. This is visualization that enables us to become the person we want to be. Visualization can work in any part of your life.

Imagination gives you the picture. Vision gives you the impulse to make the picture your own.

Robert Collier

Chapter 29

What You See is What You Get

We all have the power of visualization, and visualization can empower any part of our lives. Visualization trains your mind. There are two types of visualization: visualization of the positive and visualization of the negative. Positive visualization is focusing on what you want to happen; negative visualization is focusing on what you are afraid will happen. Only visualize the positive. You can visualize anything you want: it's a free world and it's your mind, your computer. Plant positive seeds and harvest a visualization of things that are desired. We can visualize good health. We can visualize ourselves happy, healthy, and full of vigor and vitality. If you are sick, visualize your blood cells changing. Visualize your white blood cells dominating the disease that is within your body. Visualize these good white blood cells as little warrior cells fighting off germs and bacteria. You can visualize yourself to health. You can see in your mind's eye a tumor reducing. Visualize your body focusing on the area of disease; visualize your body correcting it. You must believe that the power that created your body has the power to heal it. If you are unable to get out of bed, you can visualize yourself getting up and moving and walking.

Christopher Reeve went through the fight of his life. His visualization of walking again and someone finding a cure for paralysis kept him positive. His visualization focused on what he wanted to happen, not what was currently happening. We have the ability to alter our lives through visualization.

To accomplish this yourself, find a comfortable place. Sit or lie down and relax. Visualize your body relaxing. First your feet, then your legs, then your torso, arms, neck, and head. Visualize yourself almost floating. Visualization is a great tool for achievement in every area of your life. Visualization is a dress rehearsal of life. Visualize what you want. Visualize what God wants for you. Visualize what your family wants for you. Visualize what you want for yourself. Visualization creates realization. Spend "5 minutes" a day visualizing. Visualize being the person that you want to be. Visualization is planting seeds for the future, planting seeds of greatness.

Oliver Wendell Holmes said, *"Many of us die with the music still in us."* Give more of yourself and you will receive more from yourself. Do not sit back and wait for your stock to rise. Plant the seeds of visualization into your lives and the lives of your family and then nature will run its course.

One person who visualized his dream and goals was Ray Kroc, the founder of McDonald's, who wrote the best-selling autobiography, *Grinding It Out*. Ray Kroc started by selling paper cups for $35 a week and playing the piano part-time to support his wife and baby daughter. He left the cup business to go into the multi-mixer business, a piece of equipment used to make milkshakes. His wife was not initially thrilled by his new venture. Despite her resistance, Ray Kroc set a goal to sell one of his mixers to every drugstore, soda fountain, and dairy barn in the nation. Mr. Kroc had a saying, an aphorism, that goes, *"As long as you are green, you are growing. As soon as you are ripe, you start to rot."*

Mr. Kroc's job led to excessive travel. On a daily basis, he had to give sales presentations and accept periodic rejections. But he had a goal, he had a quest. Away from his wife and his family, he ventured forth and he sacrificed. On his quest he was told of the legendary McDonald brothers from San Bernardino, California. The McDonald brothers were turning out 40 milkshakes at a time. So, off Kroc went to San Bernardino to investigate. After observing the quality assembly line production of burgers, French fries, and milkshakes, he was amazed by the amount of business generated at one location.

If someone is doing something bigger and better than you, do not envy—emulate. Go and learn. It has been said, *"When the student is ready, the teacher will appear."* Kroc approached the McDonald brothers and said, *"Why don't you open other restaurants like this?"* They objected, saying, *"It would be a lot of trouble and we don't know who we'd get to open it."* The person they got was none other than Ray Kroc.

Sounds simple and easy—but nothing is. Ray Kroc went on to say, *"When I flew back to Chicago that fateful day in 1954, I had a freshly-signed contract with McDonald brothers in my briefcase. I was a battle-scarred veteran of the business wars, but I was still eager to go into action. I was 52 years old. I had diabetes and insipient arthritis. I had lost my gallbladder and most of my thyroid gland in earlier campaigns. But I was ahead of myself. I was still green and growing."*

While Ray Kroc felt green, the McDonald brothers acted ripe. They didn't want it to work or put in the effort, so they asked for 2.7 million dollars for a buyout. Ray Kroc borrowed the money, as he was not yet affluent and money was scarce. He had to give up one half of 1% for a period of time to facilitate the loan. The final cost of the McDonald's Corporation was 14 million dollars and the McDonald brothers took their 2.7 million dollars and went fishing. Ray Kroc was now 57 and leaner than ever. McDonald's continued to grow. Today, McDonald's is a multibillion dollar company. Ray Kroc, starting at 52, was able to build McDonald's into a billion dollar company in 22 years. It took IBM 46 years to reach a billion dollars in revenues and Xerox took 63 years. We must grind it out.

Destiny is not a matter of chance—it's a matter of choice. Ray Kroc proved two principles:

    1. It's never too late.   2. Success takes time.

The McDonald brothers' heirs must wonder what their 2.7 million would be worth today. I'm sure the McDonald family regrets selling their franchise at such a low price. It's the grinders, not the quitters, who end up the winners.

From Shakespeare's *Julius Caesar*, *"There is a little tide in the affairs of men. Which, taken at the flood, leads on to fortune; omitted, all the voyage of their life is bound in shallows and miseries. On such a full sea are we now afloat, and we must take the current when it serves, or lose our ventures."*

Ralph Waldo Emerson said, *"The reward of a thing well done is to have done it."* In order to succeed, we must grind it out. Dave Thomas, the founder of Wendy's, was an orphan. Colonel Sanders did not stake his claim until he was in his 60s. Both of these men might have had a different recipe, but they utilized the same formula—an innate desire and propensity to succeed. These men never feared failure, they embraced life and ground it out. Even a tortoise cannot move forward until it sticks its head out of its shell. We learn from these fast-food magnates that success might not come swiftly, but through hard work, visualization, and realization, we can create actualization. Spend "5 minutes" a day grinding it out.

I have about concluded that wealth is a state of mind, and that anyone can acquire a wealthy state of mind by thinking rich thoughts.

Andrew Young

Chapter 30

Heads Up—The Power of the Mind

Edmund Spenser said it best when he said, *"It is the mind that maketh good or ill, that maketh wretch or happy, rich or poor."*

The force of talent that triumphs becomes belief, unharnessed and prodded in a positive direction. The feats that can be accomplished are infinite. It's our belief that can turn the impossible to the possible. Conversely, belief can turn the possible to impossible. I am of the belief that your belief, your choice, controls your destiny.

In Haitian culture, a person's belief in the deadly power of the witch doctor "pointing the bone" can indeed cause death. But the real killer is the belief, the fear, the uncertainty, not the witch doctor.

In our life we have had positive and negative expectations. The outcome of these expectations has had an effect on our present circumstances and belief system. So often people blame events, circumstances, or developments for how their lives turned out. Yet, what really shapes our lives is the meaning we attach to the events, circumstances, and developments.

James Allen, who wrote *As a Man Thinketh*, said, *"We cannot control our circumstances, but we can control our thoughts."* Thoughts will create new circumstances. Thoughts are synonyms to beliefs. Beliefs have the ability to create destiny. Remember, nothing in life has meaning unless we give it meaning. The American Heritage Dictionary defines belief as *"trust or confidence, a conviction or opinion."* Therefore, a belief is a feeling of certainty.

Sophocles said, *"Heaven never helps the man who will not act."* I want you to adopt the belief that reading should be your window to the world and act on that belief. Reading is a way that you can alter your belief system. Harry Truman said, *"Not all readers are leaders, but all leaders are readers."* Recognize that great leaders have a belief system. Edison believed, even after failing over a thousand times while attempting to create the filament and the light bulb, that he would succeed.

What is the secret to success? It starts with the basis of a belief system—a belief in yourself, a belief with conviction. Recently, Forbes magazine came out with a profile of the richest man in America, Bill Gates. Bill Gates' career was launched as a college student at Harvard University. It was there that he committed to software, software that he had yet to develop for a computer he had never seen. Bill Gates' unyielding belief in himself led him to the top of his industry.

Mahatma Gandhi personifies a different kind of success. He believed he could gain autonomy for India by peacefully and non-violently opposing Great Britain, something that had never been done before. He wasn't being realistic, but he certainly proved to be accurate.

Believe in yourself, for your beliefs will determine your future personally and professionally. Beliefs can begin with affirmations. We studied affirmations beginning in Chapter 5. In review, affirmations are really nothing more than positive self-talk. They are positive statements made to you by yourself. While talking to ourselves we are building ourselves up, increasing our beliefs. Remember some of my examples, *"I am healthy, I am happy, I am successful, I am liked, I am loved, and I am a valuable individual."* It's important that we spend "5 minutes" a day introducing your brain to the value of affirmation. Affirmations create beliefs, and beliefs will improve and increase self-esteem.

Remember, an affirmation can be any positive statement we tell ourselves when we want to achieve or, putting it in the present, "when" we have achieved. Starting with the word *"I"* gives more power to any affirmation.

Example:

> *I* now have health.
>
> *I* now weigh 180 pounds.
>
> *I* am doing great.
>
> *I* am happy.
>
> *I* am successful.

I AM is the most powerful statement that we can use. I AM is the key to an inner belief system. I AM in control of my destiny. I AM the author of this book. I AM happy. I AM proud. I AM successful. I AM doing my affirmations while you read them.

"5 Minute" To Shake It Off And Step Up

A parable is told of a farmer who owned an old mule. The mule fell into the farmer's well. The farmer heard the mule braying (or whatever mules do when they fall into wells). After carefully assessing the situation, the farmer sympathized with the mule, but decided that neither the mule nor the well was worth the trouble of saving. Instead, he called his neighbors together and told them what had happened and enlisted them to help haul dirt to bury the old mule in the well and put him out of his misery.

Initially, the old mule was hysterical! But as the farmer and his neighbors continued shoveling and the dirt hit his back a thought struck him. It suddenly dawned on him that every time a shovel load of dirt landed on his back—he should shake it off and step up! This he did, blow after blow.

"Shake it off and step up... shake it off and step up... shake it off and step up!" he repeated to encourage himself. No matter how painful the blows, or how distressing the situation seemed, the old mule fought panic and

just kept right on shaking it off and stepping up.

You're right! It wasn't long before the old mule, battered and exhausted, stepped triumphantly over the wall of that well. What seemed like it would bury him, actually blessed him, all because of the manner in which he handled his adversity.

That's life. If we face our problems and respond to them positively, and refuse to give in to panic, bitterness, or self-pity, the adversities that come along to bury us usually have within them the potential to benefit and bless us. Remember that forgiveness, faith, prayer, praise, and hope are all excellent ways to SHAKE IT OFF AND STEP UP out of the wells in which we find ourselves.

We, as human beings, talk to ourselves constantly. But most of the time we tell ourselves what we can't do, not what we should do or what we are capable of doing. Most of the time we are saying why we are failing, why we are not succeeding, why nobody likes us, why we have no money, why we have no friends. In other words, self-talk is often negative. Therefore, we can affirm negative influences into our body as well as positive.

Regardless of your age or position in life, your attitude determines your altitude, how high you want to go in life. Let me share this story from Oprah:

In April, Maya Angelou was interviewed by Oprah (on her show) for Dr. Angelou's 74th birthday. Oprah asked her what she thought of growing older. And, there on television, she said it was exciting. Regarding body changes, she said there were many, occurring every day—like her breasts. *"They seem to be in a race to see which will reach my waist first,"* she said. The audience laughed so hard they cried.

Dr. Angelou also said, *"I've **learned** that no matter what happens, or how bad it seems today, life does go on, and it will be better tomorrow."*
*I've **learned** that you can tell a lot about people by the way they handle these three things: a rainy day, lost luggage, and tangled Christmas tree lights.*
*I've **learned**, that regardless of your relationship with your parents, you'll miss*

them when they're gone from your life.

*I've **learned** that making a "living" is not the same thing as making a "life."*

*I've **learned** that life sometimes gives you a second chance.*

*I've **learned** that you shouldn't go through life with a catcher's mitt on both hands; you need to be able to throw something back.*

*I've **learned** that whenever I decide something with an open heart, I usually make the right decision.*

*I've **learned** that even when I have pains, I don't have to be one.*

*I've **learned** that every day you should reach out and touch someone. People love a warm hug or just a friendly pat on the back.*

*I've **learned** that I still have a lot to learn.*

*I've **learned** that people will forget what you said, people will forget what you did, but people will never forget how you made them feel."*

Make your affirmations, or self-talk, positive. Have a positive belief system, fueled by positive affirmations. It sets the stage to your subconscious and superconscious mind for whatever you want to achieve, or do, or have, because it's telling yourself over and over again, in a positive statement, what you have achieved, that you are worthwhile, that you are somebody important, that you are special, that you are unique. Use affirmations daily. Take the negative self-talk that you've been using and turn it into something positive. Many people like to put affirmations on tape to hear their own voice while driving their car or relaxing at home. It's my recommendation that you say your affirmations when you wake up in the morning and when you go to bed at night. It's also positive to do your affirmations during the day. If someone is yelling at you, affirm your belief in yourself. *"I am positive, I am confident, I am not going to take these negative remarks personally."*

Use affirmations to build your positive self-esteem. Your subconscious mind doesn't know the difference between something that is synthetic and something that is real. When you tell your subconscious mind over and over again, "I am healthy, valuable, wealthy, and successful," it believes you are. You may think the opposite of yourself because your self-esteem is low, but if you tell yourself these things long enough, hard enough, and often enough with conviction, your subconscious mind will start to believe it and you'll become a positive, valuable, worthwhile, and happy person with convictions and beliefs. You will develop a positive, loving belief system. This belief system will create an aura of confidence around you. Remember, it might only take "5 minutes" a day to do your affirmations.

List 10 qualities that you like about yourself. People who succeed are people who think they can succeed. We must have a core belief system, one system that believes not only in the person that we are, but the person we are becoming.

Living In Palm Beach Florida, I am blessed to share my life with many successful people. If I didn't practice in Palm Beach County, I may never have been one the Trump's family doctors. I was blessed to have him on the cover of my first book *Lifestyle Of the Fit And Famous*. He's only one of many people that I've been blessed with through the years.

Each of the following men share the qualities of successful men that I include in my Top Ten Success Traits listed below. Each of the men I list live directly or indirectly from this code and I've learned from them. These successful men include Peter Brock, Andy Brock, Bill Meyer, Dr. Perry Bard, Dr. Harold Rosen, Dr. Glen Zuck, Joe Littenberg, Joe Jillson, Dr. Michael Axelrod, Jack Goldberger, Dr. Lee Friedel, Dr. Warren Zwecker, Tom Beechler, Jerry Alphonso, Chris O'Byrne, Ted Brooks, Tom Ness, Thomas Dougherty, Richard Bernstein, Bob Bernstein, Ira Sherman, Duane Clemons, Rabbi Joel Levine, Jerome Levine, Richard Paladino, Richard Kaufman, John Preston, Dr. Gerry Mattia, Larry Rubin, Carlos Becerra, John Fragakis, Dr. Dennis Egitto, Steven Kaplan, Moe Tarkinow, Dr. Richard Harvey, Mitch Beers, Thomas Dougherty, Dr. Robert Burke, Bruce and Steve Garfunkel, Thomas McMillen, and Richard Lubin, and Dr. Fabrizio Mancini, to name just a few. All of these men are leaders in their prospective fields.

"5 Minute" Traits of Successful People

1. **They work hard.** They're dedicated to being successful. They get up early, they rarely complain, and they expect the best from all those around them, but they demand more of themselves. To be successful, recognize that hard work pays off. And yes, they play hard, too.

2. **They're always working to improve themselves and are eager to learn.** Successful people study often, ask questions, and read constantly. While most of them did well in school, they do not rest on their laurels. Many learned more *out* of schools through experience and then continued to study and take classes and seminars regularly. I tell both my sons that continued success is not just about memorizing facts, it's about being able to take information and create, build, or apply it in new and innovative ways. Successful people want to learn everything about everything. Successful people realize that the road to success is always under construction.

3. **They know how to network and listen.** Successful people network. They love to be challenged, ask questions, and meet and correspond with other people. Their universe consists of many people, and they know many different kinds of people. They listen to friends, neighbors, co-workers, and bartenders. They understand the old saying that "even a clock that doesn't work is right twice a day." For this they listen to everyone on everything. Successful people have a database full of people who value their friendship and they always return their calls and emails.

4. **They never quit.** While the overnight sensations often

become arrogant and quickly fade from the public arena, really successful people work on every facet of themselves—their personality, leadership skills, management skills, and every other detail of life. When a relationship or business deal goes sour, they assume full responsibility. Successful people learn from everything and turn failures into future successes. Remember how Walt Disney went bankrupt numerous times. Successful people don't tolerate flaws; they fix them.

5. **They're very creative.** They do more then ask *why*, they go around asking *why not*. They see new challenges, new possibilities, new opportunities and new challenges where unsuccessful people see problems or limitations. They wake up in the middle of the night yelling, "I've got it!" They ask for advice, they experiment, they consult experts, and they're always looking for a better, faster, and more economical solution. Successful people are not just about the stuff they own; successful people create stuff!

6. **They take responsibility.** Incredibly successful people don't worry about blame, and they don't waste time complaining. They make decisions and move on. Extremely successful people take the initiative and accept the responsibilities that go with success.

7. **They always keep their composure.** Golf will tell you much about a person. The stress of a short putt for $5 can make a grown man cringe. What I've learned from these men, is they look forward to the challenge and embrace the competition. Even in times of stress or turmoil, highly successful people keep their balance and composure. They know the value of love, friendship,

humor, timing, and patience. They rarely panic or are eager to make decisions on the spot. Successful people breath easily, ask the right questions, and make sound decisions, regardless of the situation.

8. **They live in the present moment.** They know that "now" is the only time they control. They understand the gift of life is the "present." They have a gift for looking people in the eye and really listening to what's said. They enjoy a fine meal or fine wine, music, or simply playing with a child. They never seem flustered, and they always get a lot done. They take full advantage of each day of their lives. Did you utilize your "5 minutes" today to set goals or use affirmations to visualize or improve yourself? Successful people don't waste time, they use it.

9. **They look and plan for the future.** They observe trends, notice changes, see shifts, and hear the nuances that others miss. They invest in gold, real estate, the stock market and in themselves and their businesses. A professional basketball player wearing Adidas is trivial, however a college player wearing them is important, the neighbor's son wearing them is interesting, and your own children demanding them is an investment opportunity. Extremely successful people live in the present with one eye on the future.

10. **They respond instantly.** When an investment isn't working, they're not scared to make changes in their business or personal portfolio. They don't believe the sky is falling when it rains. They don't panic and are quick to respond to any challenge on any given day. When they see an opportunity, they invest the time and energy to make it work. If an important relationship is cooling

down, they take time to warm it back up. When a new competitor or a change in the economic world requires an adjustment, they are the first and quickest to respond. Steve Jobs took Apple back to the top with the iPod, iPhone, and iPad. He was always giving the public what they wanted and more. He was always quick to respond and his success is legendary.

I believe I each and every one of can utilize these traits, that we are each responsible for opening up our minds as well as the minds of other people. I believe I AM in control of my destiny. Let's choose to be successful...

Let's work hard and do it today.

Let's live in the moment.

Let's set goals today.

Let's recite our affirmations today.

Let's take responsibility for our lives today.

Let's never quit.

Let's commit ourselves to overcome any and all adversities in our life.

Let's network more and complain less.

Let's dedicate ourselves to developing a winning belief system.

Let's develop an attitude that will carry us to the top.

Remember, there's no better time than now and no better place then here, now, today. Affirm to develop the traits of success and allow your Inner Winner to work. Spend the next "5 minutes" stretching your mind, setting goals, studying, and committing to my traits for your success.

The greatest use of a life is to spend it for something that will outlast it.

Anonymous

Chapter 31

The Wisdom (or Wizard) Within

We are all brilliant. We are all surrounded by abundance.

We all have things that go right for us every day; it's just that sometimes we don't notice. This chapter is about dehypnotizing yourself so that you can go enjoy the day. This chapter is about you, your goals, your purpose, and your happiness. It's about figuring out what you love to do and doing it. This will create peace of mind. We are all guided by our inner innate intelligence. This is the wisdom within, the magical entity of our spirit that can turn fantasy into reality.

We may skip along the yellow brick road of life looking for the answers, looking for a heart, looking for courage, looking for a new body. Yet, the answers are not provided by the man behind the curtain. The answers are provided by the wisdom within. Richard Bach, the author of the best-selling books *Illusions* and *Jonathan Livingston Seagull*, said, *"What the caterpillar calls the end of the world, the master calls a butterfly."*

There is the age-old story of two caterpillars socializing on a rock when a butterfly happens to fly by. *"Did you see that?"* says one caterpillar to the other. *"I'll tell you what,"* says the other caterpillar, "you'll never catch me up in one of those things."

Not far away, standing on the edge of a cliff, a person was watching that same butterfly. Suddenly the ground gave way under her feet. After falling a hundred feet, she grabbed a rope that happened to be tied to a tree trunk and she held on for dear life. Looking down she saw that there was still a long way to go, so she looked up and yelled as loud as she could, *"Is anyone up there?"*

The clouds parted and a shaft of golden light descended to envelop her. Emanating from the heavens above came a thunderous voice, *"I AM HERE."*

"Can you help me?"

"WILL YOU OBEY MY COMMANDMENT WITHOUT QUESTION?"

"What do you want me to do?" she asked.

*"**LET GO OF THE ROPE**!"* said the voice.

For a long time, she hung there just thinking. Finally, she looked up to the heavens again and yelled, *"Is anyone else up there?"*

Now is not only the time to hang on and not let go, but now is the time to climb the rope.

Nothing is impossible.

Those who can see the invisible can do the impossible.

Disney World was not completed until after the death of Walt Disney. Shortly after the theme park's opening, a person was trying to solicit a remark from his host, Mrs. Disney. *"It's a shame that Walt did not live to see this wonderful park,"* commented the guest. Mrs. Disney replied, *"He did see it, that is why it's here today."* Walt Disney trusted his wizard within, knowing that it could create unlimited potential.

We procrastinate because:

1. We are not prepared.

2. We see something as being unpleasant, difficult, or boring.

3. We don't feel the problem loudly enough yet.

4. We don't have enough time to do it now.

5. We allow other people to talk us into procrastinating.

We can overcome it by:

1. Planning ahead.

2. Making things creative or fun.

3. Using preventative maintenance before the squeaking begins.

4. Taking advantage of small bits of time (such as "5 minutes" a day).

5. Being decisive.

6. Contacting the wizard within.

Did you know that *The Wizard of Oz* was originally banned in parts of the United States because it was considered to be a threat to society and an invitation to anarchy? I found this amazing when I first read this. Coming from a complex home, movies like *The Wizard of Oz* were my favorite means of escape. How could this movie, this classic, possibly be banned, you may ask? How could this happen? What was the rational or reasoning behind such censorship? How could such a beautiful and fun story be considered sacrilegious? The reason was that the story (which led us to the discovery that the wizard was simply a human being) taught that each individual had the power within them to create their desires, and no authority figure was needed to grant these desires. Are you getting the picture, now?

First and foremost, there was a spiritual side to this story. Each of the characters felt that there was something that they lacked that would be vital for their journey:

The Scarecrow needed a brain.

The Cowardly Lion needed courage.

The Tin Man needed a heart.

Dorothy wanted to get home.

However, through their journey, the circumstances that were created enabled them to draw on their innate ability within to prove that everything they needed was already there. One great example was the Scarecrow, my favorite. The Scarecrow thought he lacked a brain, yet he devised a strategy to outwit the Wicked Witch. The Tin Man thought he lacked heart, yet he cried so hard that he rusted. The Cowardly Lion turned out to be the hero of the story—he displayed a courage he always felt he lacked. What a great message this offers to everyone. All the tools for greatness, regardless of our insecurities, are already present.

The movie was as much about the trials and tribulations they faced along the Yellow Brick Road as the conclusion where each character found themselves. Once they got to Oz to seek the Wizard's advice and support, they realized that the Wizard was no more than a human being and had no greater powers than then any of the other seekers. The Wizard was only a source of motivation. He reminded the seekers that they always had everything they needed to create their heart's desires within from the beginning. The Wizard reminded them to call on the innate power within, just as they had done when traveling through the adversities of their journey. Remember how they defeated the witch? How about those flying monkeys?

The Wizard's role was to remind the characters—the seekers of wisdom, strength, and knowledge—that they had always possessed the power to create everything they needed, and it was an illusion to rely on someone or something outside of themselves. The Wizard redirected them to The Wizard Within, a magical source that each and every one of us possess. Many consider this the voice that talks to them during the day, I consider it an inner intelligence, guided by our subconscious and directly connected to the power of life.

The story of the *Wizard of Oz* is rich in symbolism. The symbol of the Wizard as a magician is a strong symbol for the illusionary thoughts and beliefs that we have that keep giving others power over us. We must look for the power of life within ourselves. We cannot constantly believe that success, health, and happiness are an outside job. Often, the continuous quest for illusions keeps us from realizing our greatest potential by opening to The Wizard Within. The Wizard Within has the intelligence, the power, to solve any and all challenges. The Wizard Within is our own personal guide, our personal source of strength that will provide us the insight, the power, and the energy to overcome every difficulty, weakness, or obstacle we may face daily. Look inside and Awaken the Wizard Within yourself and feel the power, the inner strength that you possess. The Wizard Within has the power to feel love and to be loved and you control this power. That alone should make you feel powerful.

The *Wizard of Oz* is based on one person's quest to find the truth. Dorothy was simply looking to get home, to get back to where she was comfortable. To Dorothy, "home" symbolized a place of unconditional love, comfort, and peace. We're all striving to find this place. This is our path. This is our journey. This is our destiny. However, this place is not someplace far away. This place of peace, comfort, and unconditional love is within us. Dorothy always had the power to go to this place, just as her fellow travelers had what they needed within them all along. Yes, each of us has the power and the strength to be anyone or anywhere, if we just look inside to The Wizard Within. Take "5 minutes" today to activate your wizard, ask yourself any question the innate power you posses will activate and inspire your Wizard.

Inside yourself you already have everything you need to accomplish anything. The secret of life, I AM, and The Wizard Within lie within each and every one of us. It's nothing more then a false illusion that something or someone outside of us must continually validate us for us to feel whole, perfect, and complete. In truth, we are whole, perfect, and complete just as we are. God, in his perfection, would not create an imperfect world or an imperfect person. Just as God has faith in us, we must have faith in ourselves.

I consider myself more of a spiritual person then a religious person. I once asked my mother, "*Who is God?*" She responded, "*God is love and love is God.*" She used to tell me the following story:

> Once upon a time, there was an island where all the feelings lived: Happiness, Sadness, Knowledge, and all of the others, including Love. One day it was announced to the feelings that the island would sink, so everyone constructed boats and left except for Love.
>
> Love was the only one who stayed. Love wanted to hold out until the last possible moment.
>
> When the island had almost sunk, Love decided to ask for help.
>
> Richness was passing by Love in a grand boat. Love said, *"Richness, can you take me with you?"*
>
> Richness answered, *"No, I can't. There's a lot of gold and silver in my boat. There's no place here for you."*
>
> Love decided to ask Vanity who was passing by in a beautiful vessel. *"Vanity, please help me!"*
>
> *"I can't help you, Love. You are all wet and might damage my boat,"* Vanity answered.
>
> Sadness was close by so Love asked, *"Sadness, let me go with you."*
>
> *"Oh, Love, I am so sad that I need to be by myself!"*
>
> Happiness passed by Love, too, but she was so happy that she didn't even hear when Love called her.
>
> Suddenly, there was a voice, *"Come, Love, I will take you."*
>
> It was an elder. So blessed and overjoyed, Love forgot to ask the elder where they were going. When they arrived at dry land, the elder went her own way.
>
> Realizing how much she owed the elder, Love asked Knowledge, another elder, *"Who helped me?"*
>
> *"It was Time,"* Knowledge answered.
>
> *"Time?"* asked Love. *"But why did Time help me?"*
>
> Knowledge smiled with deep wisdom and answered, *"Because only Time is capable of understanding how truly valuable Love is."*

The simple reality is we are beautiful, powerful, strong, intelligent, capable, lovable, and acceptable just as we are. We have the time and power to change our lives in an instant. Now I am asking you to spend the next "5 minutes" looking in the mirror and seeing the strength and power that exists within you. You have the power to heal pains from the past, just by letting go. You have the power to create the life you always dreamed of. This power is given to us by The Wizard Within. With love in our heart we empower our Wizard Within. Fill your heart with love. It's your job to activate this Wizard, here, now, today. It will be the best "5 minutes" you ever spent.

Once you understand how powerful you are within, you exponentially increase the power and potentiality of everything outside of you.

Steve Maraboli

Chapter 32

The Power of One

We must all recognize that life begins with one sperm and one egg united, that we on this planet are given one life, one day at a time, each day consisting of 86,400 seconds. We live in one body with one brain, one heart, one conscious, one subconscious, and one superconscious.

Oliver Wendell Holmes once attended a meeting in which he was the shortest man present.

"Dr. Holmes," quipped a friend, *"I should think you'd feel rather small among us big fellows."*

"I do," Holmes retorted, *"I feel like a dime amongst pennies."*

What causes us to reach our potential? I believe that there are three components that work together: physical, chemical, and emotional.

What is it within a person that pushes them to their limits? I am proud that I jog 10–12 miles a week. Mentally I feel in good shape, considering I've had multiple surgeries, osteoarthritis, sometimes have difficulty going to sleep, and sometimes have even more difficulty getting out of bed. Yet, through habit, I force myself to move on, knowing that although my joints may be weak, my heart will remain strong. I know that my brain will control my body.

Although this is an amazing task for some people, it's eclipsed by the accomplishments of Stu Mittleman. Mittleman broke the long distance record, running over 1,000 miles in 11 days and 19 hours, averaging 84 miles per day. What allowed him to stretch his body to these limits? The power of himself. It's amazing what we are capable of doing when we put our body, mind, and soul into it. A bell is not a bell unless you ring it. A song is not a song unless you sing it. A life is not a life unless you live it. Live your life. Recognize the power that you have. Abraham Lincoln said, "The best thing about the future is that it comes one day at a time, one second at a time, and one minute at a time." Life starts with one, but it does not finish there; it only begins there. Don't underestimate yourself or the power of one's self.

The greatest thing about life is not so much where we are, but in which direction we are moving. It's time for us to make our move—we *must* make our move. When the sun rises in Africa, the gazelle starts running, for if it doesn't, the lion will eat it for lunch. When the sun rises in Africa, the lion starts running, for if it doesn't catch the gazelle, it will starve to death. The moral of the story is that when the sun comes up, no matter what your position, you'd better start running. If you don't, you will either starve or be eaten.

Here is one of my favorite passages from *The Power of One* by Bryce Courtney:

> He would often use an analogy from nature. "Ja, Peekay, always in life an idea starts small, it's only a sapling idea, but the vines will come and they will try to choke your idea so it cannot grow and it will die and you will never know you had a big idea, an idea so big it could have grown thirty metres through the dark canopy of leaves and touched the face of the sky." He looked at me and continued, "The vines are people who are afraid of originality, of new thinking; most people you encounter will be vines, when you are a young plant they are very dangerous." His piercing blue eyes looked into mine. "Always listen to yourself, Peekay. It's better to be wrong than simply to follow convention. If you are wrong, no matter, you have learned something and you will grow stronger. If you are right you have taken another step towards a fulfilling life."

"5 Minutes" of Practice + Preparation = Positive Results

You must recognize your potential. You must reach your potential. The clock is always ticking. Life does not offer time-outs on health or success. In life there are two ways to learn anything: by personal experience or by other people's experience.

It's for this that we study history throughout our years of school. We study history so we can learn from the successes and failures of our world's past. I was once asked, *"What can you learn from failure?"* My reply was, *"I can learn what not to say, not to do, and not to believe. Why emulate someone or something which has failed?"*

In ancient Athens, Greece, a young man named Demosthenes, by asking to speak to the leader of Athens, stepped into the spot that some of the greatest orators in history have occupied. His voice was weak and faltering, his manner timid, and his thoughts muddled. Also, he spoke with a stammer. When he finished, the crowd booed and hissed him off the platform. But Demosthenes was not to be held down. *Never again will I speak unprepared,* he promised himself, and prepare he did. He cultivated his voice by shouting at the top of his lungs. He practiced his speech under a dangling sword to bolster his courage. He practiced for hours on end with pebbles in his mouth to eliminate his stammer. He prepared his speeches so well that he was often accused of over-preparing them. The next time he addressed an assembly, he was a different man with eloquent words, powerful words, powerful voice, and a stately manner. He drew uproarious cheers from his audience.

How could a faltering, stage-frightened, stammering man rise from rejection and failure to become one of the greatest orators in Greek history? The answer lies in one word—preparation. We learned in the last chapter that within each and every one of us lies a Wizard. This Wizard manifests itself as that little voice that always talks to us and tells us what to do and what not to do. Some call it a conscious, some call it a subconscious, and some call it a superconscious. This little wizard within us, this little voice that talks into our ear every day—this voice can guide us. This voice can alter our destiny. This voice can unlock the chains that have been harnessing us from reaching our potential. You see, Demosthenes knew his first speech didn't rule his destiny. With true preparation, he developed the ability, through ability he developed self-confidence, through self-confidence he developed a better self-image, and through a better self-image he was able to be the best that he could be.

Beethoven rose above deafness to compose majestic music. Stevie Wonder rose above blindness to sing his songs. Helen Keller, who could not see, hear, nor speak, carved her place in history as a motivator, as an author, and as a human being. An editor told Louisa May Alcott that she had no writing ability and that she should forget about attempting it—the classic book *Little Women* came shortly thereafter. Thomas Edison never made it through high school, yet I am sure that even Steven Spielberg gives thanks for Edison's many marvelous inventions. When Walt Disney submitted his first drawings for publication, the editor told him he had no talent, especially when it came to drawing animals.

We must understand that success comes from within. One equation for success is:

$$1T + 4D = S$$

Talent + Desire + Dedication + Discipline + Determination

= Success

Spend the next "5 minutes" writing this formula down. Keep it in your wallet and anytime you are looking for the formula to success just pull it out and let its dynamics go to work.

"5 Minute" Success Tips

1. Desire. How much do you want it? What price are you willing to pay? Do you want to succeed or need to succeed? Do you wish for success, or do you desire success at all costs? Are you willing to sacrifice for success? Desire is a relentless need to succeed.

2. Dedication. Athletes train every day, pushing their bodies to the limit. Actors train every day, pushing their brains to the limit. Are you willing to pay the price? Are you willing to get up "5 minutes" early and stay up "5 minutes" later? The difference between ordinary and extraordinary is the extra. Are you giving the extra? Give the extra.

3. Discipline. Are you disciplined in your discipline? Are your habits healthy habits? Do you give your minimum, yet want the maximum? Do you give your maximum expecting the minimum? Do you control your destiny or does your destiny control you? Control your destiny.

4. Determination. Are you determined to succeed? Will you pay the price that needs to be paid? Will obstacles detour you or will you detour obstacles? Detour your obstacles.

5. Success. A culmination of our visions, dreams, desires, dedication, discipline, and determination, all paid for with the currency of desire. We must be content because we are successful, and we are successful when we are content.

Now is the time to institute the four Ds in your life. This has never been more urgent. Remember, winners do what losers don't find time to do. The formula for success is simple, but following it and implementing it will take no more than "5 minutes" a day. Lets spend the next "5 minutes" implementing this formula into our lives. The time will be well spent. The success will then be earned.

Action is the foundational key to all success.

Pablo Picasso

Chapter 33

If I Can Do It, You Can Too

I began life, literally, with nothing. I was given up as an infant by my biological mother, who was a young, unmarried woman from the small town of Mustula in Saskatchewan, Canada. A poor, middle-aged couple, John and Mary Linkletter, adopted me. My adoptive father was one of the warmest men I have ever known, but he had absolutely no ability as a businessman. A part-time evangelical preacher, he also tried selling insurance, running a small general store, and making shoes, all rather unsuccessfully. Eventually we found ourselves living in a charity home run by a local church in San Diego. Then, Dad Linkletter felt called by God to become a full-time preacher, and we had even less money. What we did have was usually shared with whatever derelict neighbor happened to be looking for a meal.

I graduated from high school early and hit the road as a hobo at the tender age of 16 with the idea of finding my fortune. One of the first things I found, however, was the wrong end of a pistol. My traveling companion and I were held up by a couple of toughs who found us sleeping in a boxcar. "Put your hands straight out and lie flat," one of the men ordered. "If this match goes out and I hear anything more, I'll shoot." As they searched our pockets and felt our medals, I wondered if money was what they wanted. I was frightened because I had heard stories of older hobos sexually attacking young boys. Just then, the match went out and was hastily relit. We still did not move! The thieves found a $1.30 on me, but missed $10 I had sewn into my coat lining. They also took $2 from my friend, Denver Fox.

The match went out again and I could tell by their hesitation that they were indecisive about something. As Denver and I lay there, inches apart in the darkness, I heard the hammer of the pistol click back and a cold chill ran down my back. I knew they were considering killing us. There was little risk for them; the rain hammering down on the outside of the boxcar would drown any noise. Frozen with horror, frozen with terror, I thought of my father and how he would have prayed for me had he known. Suddenly, fear left me and peace and calm returned. As if in response to my own restored self-assurance, they moved back toward us. Then I could feel one of the men push something against my arm. "Here's your thirty cents," he said. "Breakfast money."

Today I can look back on 45 years as a star of two of the longest running shows in broadcasting history. I can reflect on the success I've had as a businessman, author, and lecturer, and I can be proud of my wonderful family life. Fifty-eight years with the same wife, five grandchildren. I mention this not to be boastful, but to encourage others who are at the lower rung of the economic ladder. Keep in mind where I started and remember, if I can do it, you can, too. Yes, you can.

Art Linkletter

The axioms I now share with you came to me from the Internet from an anonymous author. Spend the next "5 minutes" reflecting on the elegance within its simplicity. Art Linkletter made people laugh, made people happy, and now it's time to smile. Enclosed are some axioms I have on the wall in my office to lighten my day. Linkletter would have embraced these axioms. I enjoy them and I hope you do, as well.

"5 Minute" Axioms for Today

- Everyone has a photographic memory. Some don't have film.

- He who laughs last, thinks slowest.

- A day without sunshine is like, well, night.

- On the other hand, you have different fingers.

- Change is inevitable, except from a vending machine.

- Back up my hard drive? How do I put it in reverse?

- I just got lost in thought. It was unfamiliar territory.

- When the chips are down, the buffalo is empty.

- Seen it all, done it all, can't remember most of it.

- Those who live by the sword get shot by those who don't.

- I feel like I'm diagonally parked in a parallel universe.

- He's not dead, he's electroencephalographically challenged.

- She's always late. Her ancestors arrived on the Juneflower.

- You have the right to remain silent. Anything you say will be misquoted, and then used against you.

- I wonder how much deeper the ocean would be without sponges.

- Honk if you love peace and quiet.

- Pardon my driving, I am reloading.

- Despite the cost of living, have you noticed how it remains so popular?

- Nothing is foolproof to a sufficiently talented fool.

- It's hard to understand how a cemetery raised its burial costs and blamed it on the high cost of living.

- Just remember, if the world didn't suck, we'd all fall off.

- The 50-50-90 rule: Anytime you have a 50-50 chance of getting something right, there's a 90% probability you'll get it wrong.

- It's said that if you line up all the cars in the world end to end, someone would be stupid enough to try and pass them.

- You can't have everything, where would you put it?

- Latest survey shows that 3 out of 4 people make up 75% of the world's population.

- If the shoe fits, get another one just like it.

- The things that come to those that wait may be the things left by those who got there first.

- Give a man a fish and he will eat for a day. Teach a man to fish and he will sit in a boat all day drinking beer.

- Flashlight: A case for holding dead batteries.

- Shin: A device for finding furniture.

- As long as there are tests, there will be prayer in public schools.

- A fine is a tax for doing wrong. A tax is a fine for doing well.

- It was recently discovered that research causes cancer in rats.

- Everybody lies, but it doesn't matter since nobody listens.

- I wished the buck stopped here, as I could use a few.

- I started out with nothing, and I still have most of it.

- When you go into court you are putting yourself in the hands of 12 people that weren't smart enough to get out of jury duty.

- Light travels faster than sound. This is why some people appear bright until you hear them speak.

There is nothing you can't do, just spend "5 minutes" today and every day, setting goals, doing your affirmations, appreciating life, and Awakening the Wizard Within.

Action speaks louder than words, but not nearly as often.
Mark Twain

Chapter 34

Act, Rather Than React

When you adhere to a system of values you will discover more productivity, harmony, fulfillment, and profitability in all areas of life. Our challenge is to clarify moral values, spiritual values, and relationship values. Some people are thermostats. These people set the temperature; these people take the initiative. Some people are thermometers. They simply react to temperatures set by others; these people respond to the standards of others.

Art Linkletter exemplifies the success of so many other great people that I have discussed throughout my book. Ray Kroc, Dave Thomas, Beethoven, Helen Keller, and Louisa May Alcott, all exemplify the power of desire, of beliefs, of visualization. Florence Chadwick knew that others had died while trying to swim the English Channel, but she did it anyway. The Wright Brothers knew that no one had ever flown before, but they didn't let that stop them. Colonel Sanders had a desire to have his own business, but despite being told he was too old, he did it anyway.

A person with a vision talks little, but does much.

A visionary person does little, but talks much.

Many other great people began life in the poorest, most humbling of backgrounds. Andrew Carnegie started work at $4 a month. John D. Rockefeller started at $6 a week. The remarkable thing was not that Abraham Lincoln was born and educated in a log cabin; the remarkable thing is that he got out. Julius Caesar was an epileptic. Napoleon was of humble parentage and far from being born a genius; he ranked 46th in his class at the academy—in a class of 65. Charles Dickens was lame and so was Handel. Homer was blind. Plato was a hunchback. Sir Walter Scott was paralyzed.

What gave these great individuals the vision, the belief, and the desire to overcome severe setbacks and become successful? Each person had an inner dream that lit a fire that could not be extinguished. *"Great visions begin as an inside job,"* Napoleon Hill said. Cherish your visions and your dreams like they are the children of your soul, the blueprints of your ultimate achievement.

Play Now, Pay Later or Pay Now, Play Later

There are two paths that each and every person may take: they can either play now and pay later or pay now and play later. Regardless of the choice, one thing is certain—life will always demand a payment. My father taught me that on the road to success there is always a sign that says, "No Free Lunch." If you do right, then you will feel good. If you feel good, then you will do right.

One of the key ingredients to success is integrity. The dictionary defines integrity as the state of being complete, unified. When you have integrity, your words and deeds match up. You will walk the walk and talk the talk. We are born with desire. We are born with motivation. We are born with integrity. Just watch a one year old try to explore and find out what is in the house. Watch this child learn to walk, learn to talk. This is natural motivation.

My observation of life is that all people who begin any endeavor or any quest, begin with the desire to succeed, but often are unmotivated by their surroundings. It's my goal to re-motivate you to participate in life. Little children want to go to school. Big children want to get out of school. Once in the working world, they want to go back to school. What is it that truly motivates or unmotivates people?

Let me give you the qualities that I believe a person must have to succeed:

1. *Positive mental attitude.* The ability to see all people and all situations in a positive way.

2. *High energy level.* Strength, stamina, and desire to work hard and never to wear down.

3. *Integrity.* Moral, honest, trustworthy, of good character.

4. *Good self-image.* Feels good about himself and makes others feel good about themselves.

5. *Leadership ability.* His belief in himself instills belief in others.

6. *Followship ability.* A willingness to submit. A team player. Willing to play follow the leader.

7. *A sense of humor.* Enjoys life. Has the ability to laugh with people and the ability to laugh at himself.

8. *Self-discipline.* Willing to pay the price.

9. *Be creative.* He must be able to see solutions, to detour the detours.

10. *See the big picture.* Able to look beyond personal interests and see the total picture.

11. *Be a student of life.* The ability to keep learning as his life keeps expanding.

Albert Einstein said, *"Try not to become a man of success, but rather try to become a man of value."*

Spend "5 minutes" today thinking about your values, the person you are, and the person you want to be. Your values will define your character. Spending only "5 minutes" per day to define your values, your

character, is a small price to pay.
Go for it now. The future is promised to no one.

Wayne Dyer

Chapter 35

The Power of Words

This is a little story about four people named Everybody, Somebody, Anybody, and Nobody. There was an important job to be done and Everybody was sure that Somebody would do it. Anybody could have done it, but Nobody did it. Somebody got angry about that because it was Everybody's job. Everybody thought that Anybody could do it, but Nobody realized that Everybody wouldn't do it. It ended up that Everybody blamed Somebody when Nobody did what Anybody could have done.

Who are you blaming for your failures in life? If you spend "5 minutes" each day working on the lessons in this book you will be motivated to reach all of your goals. Don't let the negative words of others stop you from your goal or rob you of your dreams.

Earlier in this book I mentioned the book *The Four Agreements*. In this book, Don Miguel Ruiz talks about the power of words, how one word might mean different things to different people. Take the word "pizza," for example. If you're from New York, you'll have a different idea of what pizza is than someone from Chicago.

When I was promoted to President and COO on Wall Street, running the prestigious weight-loss company Nutrisystem, at my first board meeting I handed out *The Four Agreements* to everyone present. I have since given the book to my sons and my wife and now I share them with you.

The Four Agreements

1. Be Impeccable With Your Word

Speak with integrity. Say only what you mean. Avoid using the word to speak against yourself or to gossip about others. Use the power of your word in the direction of truth and love.

2. Don't Take Anything Personally

Nothing others do is because of you. What others say and do is a projection of their own reality, their own dream. When you are immune to the opinions and actions of others, you won't be the victim of needless suffering.

3. Don't Make Assumptions

Find the courage to ask questions and to express what you really want. Communicate with others as clearly as you can to avoid misunderstandings, sadness, and drama. With just this one agreement, you can completely transform your life.

4. Always Do Your Best

Your best is going to change from moment to moment; it will be different when you are healthy, as opposed to sick. Under any circumstance, simply do your best, and you will avoid self-judgment, self-abuse, and regret.

Words have more than meaning, they have power. The power of the word is as effective as any sword. Words can cut you up and tear you down, your choice. But there is more: being true to your word is germane to building character. The essence of building character, the essence of this book, is teaching you to like yourself and to realize that you are capable of anything you put your mind to.

We need to get off the sidelines and into the game of life. Novelist

Sinclair Lewis was supposed to deliver an hour-long lecture to a group of college students who planned to be writers. Lewis opened his talk with a question:

"How many of you really intend to be writers?"

All hands went up.

"In that case," said Lewis, *"my advice to you is to go home and write."*
With that, he left.

It only takes "5 minutes" to set your goals, state your affirmations, and pursue your dreams. Life is not just about reaction, but action. We need to take action, Ruiz stated,

"God is life. God is life in action. The best way to say, "I love you, God," is to live your life doing your best. The best way to say, "Thank you, God," is by letting go of the past and living in the present moment, right here and now. Whatever life takes away from you, let it go. When you surrender and let go of the past, you allow yourself to be fully alive in the moment. Letting go of the past means you can enjoy the dream that is happening right now."

So many of us are held back by our fears, our self doubts. We need to step up to get up. If we are to live our lives, we need to live. Life, as I said, is for living, loving, laughing, and learning, not just whining, worrying, and working. The one thing I promise you about life is that you will not get out of it alive. Choose to live today.

"Death is not the biggest fear we have; our biggest fear is taking the risk to be alive—the risk to be alive and express what we really are."

Spend "5 Minutes" Each Day

Spend "5 Minutes" each day to be strong and allow nothing to disturb your peace of mind;

Spend "5 Minutes" each day to talk health, happiness, and prosperity to every person you meet;

Spend "5 Minutes" each day to make all your friends feel special;

Spend "5 Minutes" each day to look at the sunny side of everything and make your dreams come true;

Spend "5 Minutes" each day to think the best, to work only for the best, and to expect to be only be the best;

Spend "5 Minutes" each day to be just as enthusiastic about the success of others as you are about your own;

Spend "5 Minutes" each day to forget the mistakes of your past and move forward to a greater future;

Spend "5 Minutes" each day to wear a cheerful smile at all times and give every living creature you meet your undivided attention;

Spend "5 Minutes" each day to give so much time to the improvement of yourself that you have no time to criticize others;

Spend "5 Minutes" each day to be too big for worry, too noble for anger, too strong for fear; and too happy to permit the presence of negative thoughts;

Spend "5 Minutes" each day to think well of yourself and to proclaim this fact to the world—not in loud words, but in great deeds;

When I was a young boy, I used to get upset when other boys made fun of me. The words about my "big ears" often made me very upset. I would go home and tell my mother and she would say, "Sticks and stones can break my bones, but words will never hurt me." I remember her saying those words when I was young to try and convince me of its truth in the face of painful words thrown my way. What I have learned over the years is words do hurt. Verbal insults, verbal abuse, and the power of words to affect your emotions and actions are well demonstrated in science. Let's forget about the past and let's build a future "5 minutes" at a time.

Lost time is never found again.

Benjamin Franklin

Chapter 36

Our Time is Running Out

A heart surgeon took his car to his local garage for a regular service where he usually exchanged a little friendly banter with the owner, a skilled but not especially wealthy mechanic.

"So tell me," said the mechanic, *"I've been wondering about what we both do for a living, and how much more you get paid than me.."*

"Yes?" said the surgeon.

"Well look at this," said the mechanic, as he pointed to the big complicated engine. *"I check how it's running, open it up, fix the valves, and put it all back together so it works good as new. We basically do the same job don't we? And yet you are paid ten times what I am. How do you explain that?"*

The surgeon thought for a moment, and smiling gently, replied, ***"Try it with the engine running."***

Remember, it's not what others may say or think about you, but what you think and say about yourself. If you've invested your "5 minutes" consistently throughout this book, you've learned to accomplish goals and empower yourself through affirmations. You've harnessed your dreams and now know it is possible to dream the "possible" dream. You've learned the only difference between possible and impossible is just two letters: "i" and "m." From this day forward promise yourself that never again will you allow thoughts or comments of discouragement change your day or your destiny.

In one recent study, scientists have found that just hearing sentences about elderly people led research subjects to walk more slowly. In other research, people who read words of loving kindness showed increased self-compassion, improved mood, and reduced anxiety.

"Don't take anything personally. Nothing others do is because of you. What others say and do is a projection of their own reality, their own dream. When you are immune to the opinions and actions of others, you won't be the victim of needless suffering."

You Are The Artist of the Spirit

Find yourself and express yourself in your own particular way. Express your love openly. Life is nothing but a dream, and if you create your life with love, your dream becomes a masterpiece of art. Remember, life is for Living, Loving, Laughing, and Learning, not just Whining, Worrying, and Working.

If you can believe that you are the artist of your own life, your own spirit, then your life is truly a masterpiece.

Spend "5 minutes" a day every day from this day forward remembering that you and only you, are the artist of your life. If you're the artist of your life, then paint the picture of who you want to be and see yourself as you want to be seen. God has handed you the tools and given you the brush of knowledge—now go to work!

Until we dedicate ourselves to change, to growth, we will never meet our potential, we will never be truly happy.

Ralph Waldo Emerson said, "*All my life I'd been looking for something, and everywhere I turned someone tried to tell me what it was. I accepted their answers, too, though they were often in contradiction and even self-contradictory. I was naïve. I was looking for myself and asking everyone except myself questions which I, and only I, could answer. It took me a long time and much painful boomeranging of my expectations to achieve a realization everyone else appears to have been born with: that I am nobody but myself.*"

I once read that a word is like a living organism, capable of growing, changing, spreading, and influencing the world in many ways, directly and indirectly through others. That is my goal through this book, for my words to penetrate your inner self, so you make a conscious effort to enhance your subconscious to awaken your superconscious.

To build your life you must begin "5 minutes" at a time to begin taking 100 percent of the responsibility for your life. You must recognize that you are in command, that you are the captain of your own ship, that life is like a game in which you are on the playing field every minute of every day for your entire life. You are the key player, the coach and the umpire all in one. In the game of life you control of the future. You must recognize just as in a game, you don't have to play but you chose to play, you chose to make it fun.

It is never too late to change, you are never too old to grow. Remember, age did not stop Ronald Reagan from becoming President of the United States. Age did not stop Kentucky Fried Chicken's Colonel Sanders, who started that "small" franchise at age 65, with his first retirement check of less than $100. Age didn't stop Ray Kroc, as you learned, from founding McDonalds. Age didn't stop George Foreman from reclaiming the heavyweight boxing championship in 1994. George did that at the unheard age of 45 after an unprecedented 10-year absence from the boxing ring. Age doesn't stop us; we stop ourselves.

Don't let your age or other people's words of discouragement stop you from accomplishing your goals or dreams. It wasn't until my first book that I truly realized the power of words, that words take on life as well as meaning. I sat and thought about words being alive and the life they take on. Then I pondered on words spoken 3,000 years ago, written down and passed through many generations, and how they still seem very alive when read or spoken today. Before the printing press, the Bible was spread by word of mouth, as only priests could own such a document, which was hand written.

To this day, as I ponder the power of the spoken word and its ability to incite and divide, to calm and connect, or to create and effect change, I am ever more cautious in what I say and how I listen to the words around me. For someone who likes to talk, this is not always easy.

Words have many meanings, and they can bring us up or knock us down. This brings me one of the most used and shortest words in the English language. It's yet another example of why people learning English, have trouble with the language because learning the nuances of English makes it a difficult language.

There is a two-letter word in English that perhaps has more meanings than any other two-letter word and that word is *up*.

It's listed in the dictionary as an adjective, preposition, adverb, noun, and verb. It's easy to understand how *up* means toward the sky or at the top of the list, but when we awaken in the morning, why do we wake *up*?

At a meeting, why does a topic come *up*? Why do we speak *up* and why are the officers *up* for election and why is it *up* to the secretary to write *up* a report? We call *up* our friends and we use it to brighten *up* a room; we polish *up* the silver, warm *up* the leftovers, and clean *up* the kitchen.

We lock *up* the house and some guys fix *up* the old car. At other times the little word has a real special meaning. People stir *up* trouble, line *up* for tickets, work *up* an appetite, and think *up* excuses.

To be dressed is one thing, but to be dressed *up* is special. And this *up* is confusing: A drain must be opened *up* because it's stopped *up*.

We open *up* a store in the morning, but then we close it *up* at night. We seem to be pretty mixed *up* about *up*!

To be knowledgeable about the proper uses of *up*, look *up* the word *up* in the dictionary. In a desk-sized dictionary, it takes *up* almost ¼ of the page and can add *up* to about 30 definitions.

If you are *up* to it, you might try building *up* a list of the many ways *up* is used. It will take *up* a lot of your time, but if you don't give *up*, you may wind *up* with a hundred or more.

When it threatens to rain, we say it's clouding *up*. When the sun comes out we say it's clearing *up*. When it rains, it wets *up* the earth. When it does not rain for awhile, things dry *up*. One could go on and on, but I'll wrap it *up*.

Words can be fun and have many meanings so don't be hurt or affected by others' words. Don't look for others' words to validate your essence, either. This comes from the The Wizard Within: your innate intelligence that has everything you need already inside of you waiting for you to take it out.

"You can have many great ideas in your head, but what makes the difference is the action. Without action upon an idea, there will be no manifestation, no results, and no reward," says Ruiz.

We understand that growth represents change and that change is good. You can change your life by changing your thoughts. If you continue to think like you have always thought, you'll continue to get what you have always gotten. Is it enough? If not, alter your thoughts and you will alter your destiny.

Life is a frame of mind; you are its carpenter. Build yourself to be the person you want to be, the person you desire to be, the person you dare to be. I dare you to reach out and touch someone. I dare you to dig in and touch yourself. Thomas Carlisle said, *"Isolation is the sum total of wretchedness to man."* Don't isolate yourself.

As you become successful, you will take others to the top with you. You will blaze new trails and do things that you have never done before. At that particular time, you will realize the power that exists within. People will be startled with the benefits. You will be startled by the benefits that were not available to you when you began. As you take others to the top with you, they will not stay if they do not deserve to be there. Free yourself from all pettiness and prejudice. Hope that all those you take to the top will find happiness and success. Set your sights on your own personal goals and let no one or nothing stand in your way; that's what it's all about. It takes character to walk that extra step, to climb that extra hill, to run that extra mile. Remember, the key is to unlock the master motivator within, and the person who is the master of human relations is priceless. Treat a person the way you want that person to treat you. Find out what other people want. Help them obtain it and you will be successful.

Within your being you have the ability to be happy, healthy, and successful. You need no other love than the one true love offered in great abundance by the One who really cares about you most—the Creator of all. Fully realize that you are a unique being with unique talents and offering unique services that are possessed by no other creature. Realize that you are deeply loved and cared for and that you have the opportunity to explore the great universal laws that are governed by unlimited opportunities that are available to you. Opportunity does not knock only for the rich and famous. Opportunity knocks for each and every one of us, each and every day; it just doesn't push the door open. Let opportunity in. By opening your mind you will open the door of opportunity. Most people allow fear to cripple their thoughts of success. It was Francis Bacon, the English philosopher and statesman, who wrote, *"A wise man will make more opportunities than he finds."* Don't be so idealistic as to think that someone is going to give you an opportunity that will make you rich and successful—people tend to keep those opportunities to themselves.

Are you willing now to invest your time, energy, and effort? If you've learned anything from this book, you've learned the power of using only "5 minutes," 300 seconds a day, to change your life. William Arthur Ward wrote:

Sing a new song; dance a new step; take a new path.

Think a new thought; accept a new responsibility; memorize a new poem.

Try a new recipe; plan a new adventure; entertain a new idea.

Learn a new language; blaze a new trail; enjoy a new experience.

Make a new friend; read a new book; see a new movie.

Climb a new hill; scale a new mountain; launch a new career.

Find a new purpose; fill a new need; light a new lamp.
Exercise a new strength; grasp a new truth; practice a new awareness.
Add a new dimension; encourage a new growth; affirm a new beginning.
Discover a new answer; envision a new image; conceive a new system.
Dream a new dream; chart a new course; build a new life.
Open a new door; explore a new possibility; capture a new vision.
Start a new chapter; seek a new challenge; express a new confidence.
Write a new plan; turn a new page; follow a new direction.
Watch a new program; be a new person; radiate a new enthusiasm.

Now is your time to be a new person and radiate a new enthusiasm. Now is your time to change and succeed. It only takes "5 minutes" a day to put yourself in the game of life. It takes "5 minutes" a day to win glorious triumphs and all you have to do is invest the time.

My goal today was to motivate you, to inspire you and fill your life with little "5 Minute Motivators" that you can implement today and every day for the rest of your life. Hopefully by now you've come to respect time and from this day forward you'll invest your "5 minutes" a day wisely. Never underestimate your own value or the value of your time.

A man from Jersey City came home from work late again, tired and irritated, to find his 7-year-old son waiting for him at the door.

"Daddy, may I ask you a question?"

"Yeah, sure, what is it?" replied the father.

"Daddy, how much money do you make an hour?"

"That's none of your business. What makes you ask such a thing?" the father said angrily.

"I just want to know. Please tell me, how much do you make an hour?" pleaded the little boy.

"If you must know, I make $20 an hour."

"Oh," the little boy replied, head bowed.

Looking up, he said, *"Daddy, may I borrow $10, please?"*

The father was furious. *"If the only reason you wanted to know how much money I make is just so you can borrow some to buy a silly toy or some other nonsense, then you march yourself straight to your room and go to bed. Think about why you're being so selfish. I work long, hard hours everyday and don't have time for such childish games."*

The little boy quietly went to his room and shut the door. The man sat down and started to get even madder about the little boy's questioning. How dare he ask such questions only to get some money?

After an hour or so, the man calmed down and started to think he may have been a little hard on his son. Maybe there was something he really needed to buy with that $10 and he didn't ask for money very often. The man went to the door of the little boy's room and opened the door.

"Are you asleep, son?" he asked.

"No, Daddy, I'm awake," replied the boy.

"I've been thinking; maybe I was too hard on you earlier," the man said. *"It's been a long day and I took my aggravation out on you. Here's that $10 you asked for."*

"The little boy sat straight up, beaming. *"Oh, thank you, Daddy,"* he yelled.

Then, reaching under his pillow, he pulled out some more crumpled bills. The man, seeing that the boy already had money, started to get angry again. The little boy slowly counted out his money, then looked up at the man.

"Why did you want more money if you already had some?" the father grumbled.

"Because I didn't have enough, but now I do," the little boy replied. **"Daddy, I have $20 now. Can I buy an hour of your time?"**

I love this story, because this is my story. My father loved me very much, but rarely had time for me. Only later in life did I realize that here was a man who worked two jobs, six days a week. A man who was strict, disciplined, and only wanted more for his family and was never about self. My father was a man who had two Purple Hearts and a Silver Star from World War II. He later became the Vice President of the International Ladies Garment Workers Union. He was a man who became president of his Temple and eventually a Mayor's aid in Jersey City. My father always worked hard, always valued time, and from this day forward valued me and my time. My father was a man who lived for **TODAY**.

I challenge you today to change your life one day at a time. The time to start is now, the day to start is **TODAY**.

TODAY is a most special day of your life, because we have never lived it before; and you will never live it again.

TODAY can be a special day, a healthy day for you—and for others—if you invest your time in others.

TODAY affirm to invest your time in others.

TODAY spend **"5 Minutes"** to make someone smile.

TODAY spend **"5 Minutes"** to express a word of kindness to someone you know, someone who needs your time.

TODAY spend **"5 Minutes"** to lend a helping hand to someone in need.

TODAY spend **"5 Minutes"** to give a word of encouragement to someone who is temporarily overcome with problems.

TODAY spend **"5 Minutes"** to share a portion of your success with others.

TODAY spend "5 Minutes" to lose yourself in service and you'll find that every day can be a special day, a triumphant day, and an abundantly rewarding day!

Age is an issue of mind over matter. If you don't mind, it doesn't matter.

Mark Twain

Chapter 37

Turning Back the Clock

Throughout our journey in this book, we decided how the power of the mind, commitment, goal setting, perseverance, and positive mental attitude can change your life. Imagine if you invested "5 minutes", only 300 seconds a day, to look better, feel younger, and be healthier. Would you make that investment? Of course you would and over the next "5 minutes" I'll show you how.

Since Christopher Columbus, man has searched for the fountain of youth. One of the sailors who sailed with Christopher Columbus on his second voyage to the New World was a man named Juan Ponce de León. When Columbus returned home, Ponce de León stayed in the New World and became the governor of what is now Puerto Rico. It was during these years that he kept hearing stories of a magical water source called the Fountain of Youth; it was said that drinking its water kept you young. Ponce de León decided that he must find this water source. Thus, the quest for the Fountain of Youth began. Now, 503 years later, we're still looking for the Fountain of Youth.

On my own path for the Fountain of Youth, I learned there are no short cuts. Imagine going for cosmetic injections and then ending up 100% paralyzed, living on a ventilator, and fighting for your life on a daily basis. Even worse, my wife was fighting the same dilemma. Often, I'm asked what I learned from my experience, I've learned that you can grow older gracefully and naturally. A 60-year-old person with a face lift still has a 60-year-old heart, liver, and lungs. You can't judge a book by its cover anymore, not when it comes to health. *Youthful aging* is an inside job. It starts each day when you wake up and spend "5 minutes" per day stretching your body, not just your stomach. We all want to live a long time, but we want our years to be happy, healthy, and meaningful. I like to call this phenomenon *youthful aging*.

Through technology and research we have a much better idea of how a person ages. Even as you read this chapter, you are experiencing aging. The fact is you are getting older by the second, by the end of this chapter you will be "5 minutes" older, yet you will be smarter and better equipped for ageless aging. The key is what you do with your time on this planet. The next "5 minutes" in this chapter (I probably only have four left) can change the way you look, feel, and age.

We start aging from the moment we cry out our first screaming breath. During our carefree childhood and through our teen years, our bodies change in stunning and comprehensive ways. If most or any of you were like me, those were not only our growing years, but our abusive years, as well. We ate what we wanted when we wanted, drank like beer was still a part of prohibition, smoked, and took our bodies for granted. Getting older doesn't have to mean the same thing as growing old. In this chapter we'll learn that aging is not the enemy, but often the enemy is our health habits and how we live our life. The good news is that modern science shows us how we can take control of the way and the rate at which we age, naturally.

Our bodies change over our lifetime. The clock moves so slowly, so gracefully, that often we don't even realize that our body clock, our endocrine system, is beginning to change. We begin to slowly age, yet we're able to still enjoy the perfection of strength and vitality that goes with youth. When we're young and vital, our brains tell us our bodies are still strong and invincible. We build for our future, work overtime, and raise a family. We have the physical and emotional health, as well as the stamina, to manage it and we still don't feel any effects of the aging process.

One day, however, we begin to realize that growing older is a drag. We want to be who we were. We want our stamina back, our invincibility back. We begin to see changes in our bodies. We feel more aches when we get out of bed in the morning and more pains when we go to bed at night. We begin to forget people's names, people you work with and see every day. As we get older, the perfection of youth now seems so long ago. We find ourselves thinking more about our mortality, though we try not to dwell on it. Often this is complicated by the loss or decline of our own aging family members and we begin to become the parents of our parents. We begin to think how we will cope with old age and how we can avoid this aging process.

It's at this time in our life that we begin to look for youth in the form of plastic surgery or medicine. We want to turn back the clock and look young and vital again. I did, and I paid an enormous price, not realizing the power to change was simply within. But this means change from a normal or acquired lifestyle. We often feel so tired in the morning that we begin to look for shortcuts. We start our day with a double espresso and often blood pressure and cholesterol medications. We have a fast food lunch that often leads to an antacid. For our afternoon pick-me-up we head to Starbucks for more caffeine to get us through the afternoon. Around 3:00 p.m. the headache creeps in, so now some aspirin or other pain reliever is added to our chemical cocktail. From all the caffeine we start to get anxiety, so we take another pill since we still have to perform. Now with all the aches, pains, and stress of the day, it's time for a few drinks to calm us down and a sleep aid to help us sleep. We are a country that looks for shortcuts; we have become the "chemical generation."

If you think I'm exaggerating, in my first book, *Lifestyle of the Fit and Famous*, I reviewed how 40% of all prescriptions are written for people 60 and older. The Citizen Health Group also stated that the average number of prescriptions given to people over 60 is 15 per year—37% of these people are taking 5 or more drugs at a time and about 20% are taking 7 prescriptions per day.

One of the common denominators of people with bad health, are bad health habits. Whether it's lack of exercise, smoking, drinking, or overeating, we have the ability to change. The best way to break a bad habit is to just drop it. We look for shortcuts to health and to *youthful aging* and often this shortcut leads us to a detour from a new healthy lifestyle. Now what if by investing "5 minutes" a day into your diet and your lifestyle you could lose weight and feel great? If you're interested in simple formulas and simple changes, keep reading.

Throughout this book we've learned that attitude is one of the keys to success. If being 100% paralyzed with botulism poisoning taught me anything, it taught me to fight. It taught me to take charge of my life and my health.

My objective in life is to make a difference in the Heath Care Crisis that we live in today. Recently, we were featured on a special by CNBC where they demonstrated that a minimum of 20% of all drugs in our country are counterfeit. Are we seeing a pattern? Drug dealers are no longer standing on street corners. The top recreational drugs in our country's college campuses are Adderall and Xanax. Now we can even go to some states and get our prescription for medical marijuana.

My wife and I were featured on the Dr. Oz Show, as my quest to expose the myths of *youthful aging* and show the world the natural alternatives that exist. To watch the excerpt, go to www.5minutemotivator.com/dying-to-be-young.

So where do we begin to turn back the clock if we're trying to look our best without going under the knife? Many of the secret ingredients to accomplish this might be right under your nose. I've read many articles by many experts who say the answer to aging gracefully can be found in the grocery store in fruits, vegetables, green tea, and a host of other healthful foods that are rich in antioxidants and other potentially age-deterring compounds. This is a good start. There is a reason they call certain foods junk foods.

"Dietary choices are critical to delay the onset of aging and age-related diseases, and the sooner you start, the greater the benefit," says Susan Moores, RD, a spokesman for the American Dietetic Association.

First, we need to better understand the foods we eat and know the good foods from the bad. Some foods and beverages contain powerful substances called phytonutrients. Many experts believe these nutrients are capable of unlocking the key to longevity. Phytonutrients, which are members of the antioxidant family, gobble up free radicals—oxygen molecules that play a role in the onset of many of the major illnesses associated with aging.

Scientists have shown that as we age we become more susceptible to the long-term effects of oxidative stress (basically the body has too many free radicals) and inflammation at the cellular level. The theory is that antioxidants and other age-defying compounds help cells ward off damage from free radicals and minimize the impact of aging.

Most recently we've learned that not only antioxidants, but other compounds in foods can also affect the aging process. These may be classified according to their impact on inflammation at the cellular level.

One doctor who has gotten a lot of recognition in *youthful aging* is Dr. Nicholas Perricone. He states, *"All foods fit into three categories: pro-inflammatory, neutral, or anti-inflammatory."*

He goes on to say, *"Age-related changes may be reversed by consuming foods and beverages that are rich in a variety of compounds, including antioxidants, and are anti-inflammatory, such as cold-water fish and richly-colored vegetables."*

According to Perricone, the foods we should avoid are classified as pro-inflammatory and can accelerate aging. He says, *"If we eat large amounts of saturated or trans-fatty acids, sugars, and starches, insulin levels surge and trigger an anti-inflammatory response and accelerate the aging process."*

Yes, the secret to better health often does not come by prescription; it comes from Mother Nature. We must stop being an obese nation; we must lose weight, detoxify our bodies, and supplement properly.

I've spent my life searching for a better and easier way to look good and feel good, to become not the person I was, but a new me, a better me, a stronger me, and I believe I've found the answer. What if I told you that one company has employed some of the greatest minds in the world on health and aging to find a solution to better life? It's time to put discouragement to rest because millions of people are changing their lives and so can you with "5 minutes" per day of good habits.

As we shift paradigms, going from a sickness model to a wellness model, we begin to focus on the cause of sickness, disease, and aging. Instead of treating symptoms that are derived when disease is already present and apparent, a wellness model attacks the cause.

Many scientific authorities are involved in the surge of exploration to discover why and how aging and disease occurs. The objective is to investigate potential methods of slowing and even reversing the aging process. Progress is made daily and research has revealed ways to prolong physiological and psychological health for both the young and old.

It's now estimated that almost one in five Americans will be diabetic. Obesity is on the rise, yet we can turn back the clock, lose weight, detoxify our system, and grow newer, healthier tissues. Researchers have been able to recognize certain aspects that control the progression of aging, as fresh information is acquired regularly and at a quick pace. There has been abundant supposition made regarding aging, but the topic is quite comprehensive and certain areas are connected.

Nutritional supplements are more important today than ever. Our bodies are forced to deal with greater environmental pollutants (impurities) and we're undernourished because over-farming has depleted the nutrients from our land and the produce grown on the land.

It's important to select vitamin supplements:

1. To replace the nutrients missing from our food.

2. Made with the highest quality raw materials.

3. Made with nutrients that enhance absorption.

4. Made with nutrients that naturally cleanse impurities.

Scientists and companies are now working on unlocking the genetic secrets of aging. Be patient with me for a moment as I walk you through a bit of the science. The conclusion is going to knock your socks off!

You already know that your cells reproduce by dividing into two new cells. From the moment of conception until the final minutes of life, the trillions of cells in your body are regenerating through this process.

Scientists have discovered that over the course of our life our cells continue to divide at will with little change in overall health and longevity. This is how the growth process unfolds: your body is constantly rebuilding, repairing, and renewing itself. Imagine if you cut yourself shaving in the morning. Your body knows exactly how to stop the bleeding and how to heal the skin, so by the next morning you and your razor are at it again.

Experts searched for why cells in older men or women—dividing by the exact same process—start slowing down over time and eventually stop dividing and die. The question arose: If the physiological process of cell division doesn't change over your lifetime, shouldn't new cells look and function the same regardless of your age?

Unfortunately, they do not. We're able to tell the difference between a newly-divided old cell and a newly-divided young cell just by looking at them under a microscope. Each new cell is not an exact copy of its parent cell. This is how we age. Still, the reason of why we age remained a mystery.

Scientists have been working on this answer over the past 50 years. The prestigious journal *Nature* published a groundbreaking article in 1990 that introduced the world to an explanation of the genetic mechanism that involves something called the telomere.

Telomeres are small stretches of protein caps at the ends of every cell's DNA. DNA is made up of two strands of long sequences of genes. They take the shape of what's called a double helix—sort of like a spiral staircase. They contain all your genetic material.

The telomeres act like the plastic fittings at the end of your shoelaces. They were previously known only for their role in healthy gene function because they keep the ends from fraying.

What the authors published in *Nature* was the new realization that the telomere is also your biological clock. Each time your cells divide, a small end portion of the telomere is not copied, making your telomeres shorter and shorter over time. Each new generation of cells has a slightly shorter telomere than its parent. Further research confirmed it. Telomeric length is now the main focus of research in *youthful aging*.

The shortening of telomeres can be slowed by relieving oxidative stress and Isagenix has a system that addresses this stress. I was first educated about Isagenix by Laura Kampfhenkel and Dr. Ted Brooks. Laura was my key person when I worked on Wall Street and we acquired 50% of Nutrisystem, the weight loss company. I am more optimistic about my participation with Isagenix than I ever was with Nutrisystem.

This isn't a commercial for Isagenix, but it *is* a testimonial. I was paralyzed while trying to look younger. I wanted to find a natural way to feel and look good, so I began my research as you also should do. I devoted "5 minutes" per day to learn more about telomeres, Isagenix, and *youthful aging*. Imagine how I felt as a doctor when I learned that Isagenix has also helped thousands of people lose an estimated 5.4 million pounds and 6.5 million inches. Those are amazing numbers in a country that is battling the war on obesity!

I learned their system was:

- Not a diet or quick-fix, it's a healthy lifestyle.

- Promotes life-long health and vitality.

- Boosts energy naturally.

- Reduces cravings for unhealthy food.

Founders John Anderson and Jim and Kathy Coover were retired when they were inspired to establish Isagenix—a company that could transform the health, wealth, and happiness of people in search of a better quality of life. They now have added their son Erik to form a dynamic triumvirate of heath. When I spoke with Kathy Coover on the phone, she shared her mission. *"Our vision is to impact world health and free people from physical and financial pain, and in the process create the largest health-and-wellness company in the world."*

Isagenix has experienced explosive growth since it's founding because our leaders bring a unique combination of nutritional and direct-marketing experience and success to the company.

People are amazed by my stamina and lifestyle. For those who have read my books, I rarely endorse any company and as a doctor I am skeptical. But Isagenix is a billion-dollar company that has helped millions of people throughout the world—for a reason. Recently I lost 5 pounds while drinking their meal replacement shakes and eating their chocolate snacks, while still enjoying my lifestyle. In "5 minutes" per day, you can lose 5 pounds or more per month. Your dedication and discipline determines your result. More importantly, by detoxifying your body and losing weight, you'll get a sense of energy and vitality you haven't felt in years.

Today, at 59 years young, I'm on the road to health again, to *youthful aging*, while living and enjoying my age. I feel better, stronger, and more vital. If we're a nation at war, at war with drugs and conventional medical care, we need to fight back with weapons of health. Isagenix provides these weapons to you and your family.

So imagine right here, right now, that you read this book and were inspired, were motivated and wanted more out of life and better health. What if you didn't know where to begin and you wanted a new life, to be healthier, to be your own boss, and to make a difference? What if Isagenix offered you that opportunity? Imagine that it only takes "5 minutes" to change your life. Right now, I challenge you to be the best you can be, to be open-minded, and to take "5 minutes" and go to www.5minutemotivator.com and find out how today is the first day of the rest of your life. By committing "5 minutes" to research Isagenix and learning about *youthful aging* and a better lifestyle, this may just be the best "5 minutes" you ever invest.

However, let me warn you, you may experience:

- Energy boost
- Consistent weight loss over time
- Reduced cravings for unhealthy food
- Improved muscle tone
- Balanced digestion

I challenge you to improve your life. The world is full of opportunities waiting to be seized and as you've seen, new ones turn up every day. The key to most of these opportunities is taking action—action fueled by desire and complemented by energy. I challenge you to take action now. I challenge you to spend "5 minutes" every day. I challenge you to decide every day to be the best you can be. Remember, the key is to not change the world, but to change yourself.

Imagine that in the Game Of Life, you own a bank account that credits your account each morning with $86,400. However, it carries over no balance from day to day. Every evening the bank deletes whatever part of the balance you failed to use during that day. What would you do? Draw out every cent, of course!

Each of us within us has such a bank account—it's called TIME.

Every morning, we receive 86,400 seconds for the day. Every night it writes off as lost whatever TIME you have failed to invest.

Life carries over no balance of TIME. It allows no overdraft. Each day it opens a fresh new account for you. Each evening it burns the remains of the day.

If you fail to utilize your daily deposits of TIME, the loss is yours.

There is no going back. There is no drawing against the "tomorrow".

You must live in the present on today's deposits. Invest it wisely so you derive the utmost in health, happiness, and success.

The clock of life is running. Make the most of today, every day. Invest your 86,400 seconds wisely and deliberately. In life you can always get more money, but time spent is lost forever.

To realize the value of ONE YEAR, ask a student who failed a grade and was held back.

To realize the value of ONE MONTH, ask a mother who gave birth to a premature baby.

To realize the value of ONE WEEK, ask the editor of a weekly newspaper.

To realize the value of ONE HOUR, ask the person holding on for his or her life.

To realize the value of ONE MINUTE, ask a person who missed their plane.

To realize the value of ONE SECOND, ask a person who just avoided an accident.

Treasure every second, every minute and every hour, of every day, for the rest of your life. Live each day as it is your last. My wife and I were as close to death as you can come, we appreciate the little things and realize life is for living. At the end of your life you only have three things that matter: your friends, your family, and your memories. During my coma, it was these three things that I held on to, that I cherished, that brought me back to life. If you were told you were going to die, how much would you pay for one more hour with your family? It is at these moments that we realize that time, not money, is life's most valuable commodity.

Live a life with no regrets and give thanks to your friends and family because they shared their time and their life with you. They believed you were someone special enough to spend their lives with you.

Remember that time waits for no one. Take our final "5 minutes" to remember:

The past is history.

The future is a mystery.

But this moment of life, right here, right now is the gift.

That is why we call it the PRESENT.

I challenge you now to appreciate your gift and make use of your present. The future is right here, right now. Take the time to write down your goals and create a personal plan of action to get what you want out of life. Invest your 86,400 seconds a day wisely. To change yourself, to change your life, it takes only 300 seconds—only "5 minutes." Don't spend another second, minute, hour, day, month, or year of your life settling for less than you deserve. Give life all you've got. Life is not only a challenge, but an opportunity. Life is complex with its paradoxes of pain and pleasure, success and failure. You just need to search within yourself. I challenge you to get excited about life. You have 86,400 seconds every day to make a difference. Use them wisely. Spend "5 minutes" a day unlocking the miracle of motivation, the power of goals, the strength of affirmations and you will awaken The Master Motivator, The Wizard Within.

The clock is ticking—go to work.

Good luck!

Bonus 1

"5 Minute" Tips for Youthful Aging

Youthful aging doesn't have to mean turning to cosmetic surgery or chemicals. If you really want to look younger and stay healthy, here are my top ten tips for *youthful aging*:

1. Quit smoking

One of the most important *youthful aging* tips of all. If I could do it, you can. If I was a smoker at the time of our injections, I would be dead. I have come to learn your lungs are everything and are just as important as your heart. Once we got off the ventilator and were able to breathe on our own, our strength returned.

If you smoke, STOP NOW. It's as simple as that. Over time, you may able to completely reverse the damage smoking has done to your skin and you'll for sure stop the damage from getting worse. With the right *youthful aging* skin care, proper nutrition, and a good multi-vitamin—you should begin to look younger and healthier than you have for years, if we could do it so could you..

Smokers do not usually have healthy skin. So, do your face, your body, your lungs a favor and quit smoking now. Kick start your cessation program with acupuncture or laser therapy. You're more likely to succeed with help than by trying to quit cold turkey.

If you do choose to continue smoking be prepared for the consequences. Smoking accelerates skin aging by encouraging the destruction of collagen. Reduced levels of collagen are one of the primary reasons your skin ages, so a smoker's skin ages much faster. The tell-tale signs are dull, grayish, dry skin, increased wrinkling around the eyes, and the puckering wrinkles from drawing on cigarettes, known as "smoker's face."

Is it really what you want for your skin?

2. Protect your skin from the sun

Sun damage is the number one enemy of younger looking skin. My friend Dr. Zwecker still yells at me on the golf course, *"Wear a hat; use sun screen."* Where did my wrinkles come from? How did I get into this mess? The sun, naturally. As a youth, I overdid it on my days at the Belmar, New Jersey beach.

Getting a suntan leads to photo-aging, a process that produces deep wrinkles in leathery textured skin and will cause premature age spots.

Use a moisturizer combined with a broad spectrum sunscreen. Always have sunscreen with you. If you want a tan—fake it—most of Hollywood does.

3. Eat a natural and high antioxidant rich diet

Antioxidants are a group of vitamins, minerals, and carotenoids that work against the damage caused by free radicals that weaken the skin's structure. For maximum *youthful aging* protection eat fresh fruit, vegetables, fruit, and whole grains. For younger looking skin make sure you get plenty of vitamins A, C, E, and Selenium; I call these my ACES. These vitamins work together to restore collagen in your skin. You also need plenty of omega-3 essential fatty acids, which will aid in a healthy heart. Omega-3s maintain the structure and fluidity of cells and help moisturize the skin from within—an essential part of your *youthful aging* diet.

4. Take a vitamin supplement for younger looking skin

Boost your antioxidant intake with a daily supplement. Go for one with the highest levels of the key vitamins and minerals for younger looking skin and all round health.

5. Add green tea to your day

Drinking green tea is an *youthful aging* tip you may not have considered. Green tea is an amazing *youthful aging* powerhouse. Recent research findings show that taking sufficient green tea during the day can protect you from all forms of cancer, build your resistance to heart disease and dementia, and contribute to your body's ability to burn fat, especially abdominal fat, resulting in possible weight loss and increased energy, even when there is no change in your daily diet. To get the wonderful *youthful aging* effects of green tea in concentrated form, take a high strength green tea powder.

6. Moisturize and exfoliate

A great *youthful aging* moisturizer, when applied properly, will provide continuous hydration—essential for mature skin—and protection from further free-radical damage. Choose the best moisturizer you can afford. Make sure it has high levels of proven effective ingredients like peptides that work to reverse the aging process and reduce wrinkles.

You have to exfoliate for younger looking skin. Without exfoliation *youthful aging* skin creams can't work their magic on the skin. Follow a disciplined and consistent skin routine and exfoliate at least twice a week to ensure that fresh, live skin is soaking up moisture. Bonnie is great at this, and I am so proud of her.

7. Exercise more

I had to learn to walk again, to utilize every muscle again, and to maintain my lungs and health. Exercise is part of my life. I don't love doing it, I love the way I feel after. Exercise is my key *youthful aging* tip. It will give you more energy, build muscle mass, increase blood flow to your skin, help prevent high blood pressure, reduce anxiety, strengthen bones, and raise your metabolic rate so you lose more weight more quickly.

With all these *youthful aging* benefits—exercise doesn't have to be a chore. Go for exercise that gives you a cardio workout as well as developing core strength and fighting abdominal, buttocks, and thigh fat. So if you haven't already, put exercise at the heart of your *youthful aging* routine.

8. Moderate your alcohol intake

My wife and I still enjoy a glass of wine. Wine is loaded with phenolic compounds and flavonoids, with a high anti-oxidant value. The key is doing it in moderation. We all know that drinking too much can lead to serious health problems. What is less talked about is the aging effect of alcohol on the skin. Alcohol is bad for your skin, as it has an inflammatory and dehydrating action that accelerates the aging process. Excess alcohol blocks the absorption of key nutrients you need for antioxidant protection. The key is drink eight ounces of water for every four ounces of wine and two ounces of regular alcohol.

9. Stress less

We are all under pressure in life. Pressure to perform, to be the best dad, best mom, best employee. We all feel the pressure to succeed. Athletes feel pressure to win. Pressure is part of life, just accept it and don't let it into your consciousness. Once you do, once you obsess over pressure, then pressure becomes stress. When you're under stress your body releases stress hormones that, over a period of time, suppress the immune system and accelerate the aging process. As a result of prolonged stress, the cells in your body—including your skin cells—are unable to regenerate properly and become more susceptible to the aging process. The result is premature lines and wrinkles. Stress really does get etched on your face.

So *youthful aging* tip number nine is to learn to recognize that pressure is okay, but stress is not, so manage it effectively.

10. Drink more water

Nothing on this planet would survive without water. Not cola—water. You need to hydrate your body, your skin, from within. Skin cells need water just like every part of your body including your brain. Without sufficient water your skin will dehydrate and essential *youthful aging* nutrients cannot be delivered to your system. You should aim to drink around eight 8-ounce glasses every day just to replace the water you lose through sweating and urination. To look good, and for a longer time, you need to make sure water is an essential part of your *youthful aging* routine.

Just about every dermatologist out there tells us we should drink water for skin health and to hydrate the skin. I did a quick review and found that respected dermatologists like Daniel Maes (Head of Research for Estée Lauder), Nicholas Perricone, Dr. Murad, and countless others less famous but no less qualified all say drinking water is important to keep skin hydrated. And hydrated skin is younger looking skin as we all know.

Loss of hydration in the skin shows in all sorts of ways—dryness, tightness, flakiness. Dry skin has less resilience and is more prone to wrinkling. Water is essential to maintain skin moisture and is the vehicle for delivering essential nutrients to the skin cells. As water is lost in large quantities every day—it stands to reason you have to replace it somehow. Drink enough water during the day to maintain the skin's moisture level. The key is to drink water throughout the day at regular intervals, this makes it easy and fun.

That's it—10 great *youthful aging* tips to help you look younger and feel great—all you need to do is spend "5 minutes" per day and follow them!

Bonus 2

"5 Minute" Lessons of Life

I share my lessons of life from my latest book, *Dying to Be Young*, published by Pegasus books and based upon an afterlife encounter. I share with you the wisdom of one of my visitors, my Uncle Herb Punyon.

1. You will receive one body. You may love it or hate it, but it will be yours for your entire life. It's the vessel that contains your spirit. If you are good to it, it will be good to you.

2. Your life is a series of lessons. You are enrolled in a full-time informal school called Life. Each day in this school you will have the opportunity to learn lessons. You may like the lessons or you may think them irrelevant and stupid. However, all days, all encounters, good or bad, will contain a lesson.

3. There are no mistakes in Life, only lessons. Growth is a process of trial and error through experimentation. The "failed" experiments are as much a part of the process as the experiment that ultimately works.

4. A lesson in Life is repeated until learned. A lesson will be presented to you in various shapes and forms until you've learned it. When you've learned it, only then can you go on to the next lesson.

5. Life's lessons never end. There is no part of your day or your life that does not contain lessons. If you're alive, there are lessons to be learned. The wise person learns from his lessons.

6. Being "there" is no better than "here." When "there" has become "here", you'll simply obtain another "there" that will look better than "here." The grass is not greener, so learn to live in the moment.

7. Others are merely mirrors of you. You cannot love or hate something about another person unless it reflects something you love or hate about yourself.

8. What you make of your life is up to you. You have all the tools and resources you need. What you do with them is up to you. The choice is yours.

9. All of life's questions and answers are inside you. All you need to do is look, listen, and trust. You must have faith in your body, your mind, your soul, and your spirit. Your inner voice and your innate intelligence will provide you with answers to all questions.

The secret of life is I AM. You harbor the strength and power of the universe.

Bonus 3

"5 Minute" Tips to Live Your Life

Don't compare your life to others. You have no idea what their journey is all about.

Don't have negative thoughts or things you cannot control. Instead, invest your energy in the positive present moment.

Don't over-do, know your limits.

Don't take yourself so seriously. No one else does.

Don't waste your precious energy on gossip.

Dream more while you are awake.

Envy is a waste of time. You already have all you need.

Forget issues of the past. Don't remind your partner of his or her mistakes of the past; that will ruin your present happiness.

Life is too short to waste time hating anyone. Don't hate others.

Make peace with your past so it won't spoil the present.

No one is in charge of your happiness except you.

Realize that life is a school and you are here to learn. Problems are simply part of the curriculum that appear and fade away like algebra class, but the lessons you learn will last a lifetime.

Smile and laugh more.

You don't have to win every argument. Agree to disagree.

Call your family often.

Each day give something good to others.

Forgive everyone for everything.

Spend time with people over the age of 70 and under the age of 6.

Try to make at least 3 people smile each day.

What other people think of you is none of your business.

Your job won't take care of you when you are sick. Your friends will. Stay in touch.

Do the right thing!

Get rid of anything that isn't useful, beautiful, or joyful.

God heals everything.

However good or bad a situation is, it will change.

No matter how you feel, get up, dress up, and show up.

The best is yet to come.

When you awake alive in the morning, thank God for it.

Your Innermost is always happy, so be happy.

Extra Bonus

Dr. Eric Kaplan's latest book:

Pillar Power:
11 Special Health Reports

I want to give you my latest book, *Pillar Power: 11 Special Health Reports.* Learn how to take control and change your health "5 minutes" at a time. Go to my website, **www.5minutemotivator.com** and sign up today. I'll send you the book right away and you'll also receive occasional tips to help you on your path to success, health, and happiness along with other bonuses.

OTHER TITLES BY DR. KAPLAN

5 MINUTES TO WELLNESS

PILLAR POWER:
11 SPECIAL HEALTH REPORTS

DYING TO BE YOUNG

LIFESTYLE OF THE FIT AND FAMOUS

SHARE YOUR MISSION

Go to www.5minutemotivator and sign up to receive your free
copy of *Pillar Power: 11 Special Health Reports*.

Made in the USA
Lexington, KY
25 June 2012